Module
1

Biblical Studies

Conversion & Calling

The Word that Creates

. . . .

The Word that Convicts

. . . .

The Word that Converts

. . . .

The Word that Calls

Capstone Module 1: Conversion and Calling Student Workbook

ISBN: 978-1-62932-001-4

© 2005, 2011, 2013, 2015. The Urban Ministry Institute. All Rights Reserved.
First edition 2005, Second edition 2011, Third edition 2013, Fourth edition 2015.

The Urban Ministry Institute is a ministry of World Impact, Inc.

Contents

About the Instructor

Rev. Dr. Don L. Davis is the Executive Director of The Urban Ministry Institute and a Senior Vice President of World Impact. He attended Wheaton College and Wheaton Graduate School, and graduated summa cum laude in both his B.A. (1988) and M.A. (1989) degrees, in Biblical Studies and Systematic Theology, respectively. He earned his Ph.D. in Religion (Theology and Ethics) from the University of Iowa School of Religion.

As the Institute's Executive Director and World Impact's Senior Vice President, he oversees the training of urban missionaries, church planters, and city pastors, and facilitates training opportunities for urban Christian workers in evangelism, church growth, and pioneer missions. He also leads the Institute's extensive distance learning programs and facilitates leadership development efforts for organizations and denominations like Prison Fellowship, the Evangelical Free Church of America, and the Church of God in Christ.

A recipient of numerous teaching and academic awards, Dr. Davis has served as professor and faculty at a number of fine academic institutions, having lectured and taught courses in religion, theology, philosophy, and biblical studies at schools such as Wheaton College, St. Ambrose University, the Houston Graduate School of Theology, the University of Iowa School of Religion, the Robert E. Webber Institute of Worship Studies. He has authored a number of books, curricula, and study materials to equip urban leaders, including *The Capstone Curriculum*, TUMI's premiere sixteen-module distance education seminary instruction, *Sacred Roots: A Primer on Retrieving the Great Tradition*, which focuses on how urban churches can be renewed through a rediscovery of the historic orthodox faith, and *Black and Human: Rediscovering King as a Resource for Black Theology and Ethics*. Dr. Davis has participated in academic lectureships such as the Staley Lecture series, renewal conferences like the Promise Keepers rallies, and theological consortiums like the University of Virginia Lived Theology Project Series. He received the Distinguished Alumni Fellow Award from the University of Iowa College of Liberal Arts and Sciences in 2009. Dr. Davis is also a member of the Society of Biblical Literature, and the American Academy of Religion.

Introduction to the Module

Greetings, dearest friends, in the strong name of Jesus Christ!

As disciples of Jesus Christ, we affirm our deep belief in the creative, convicting, converting, and calling power of the Word of God. To understand the wonderful blessing of conversion and calling, we will need to critically evaluate the place of the Word of God in the Church.

Our first lesson, *The Word that Creates*, explores the nature of the Holy Scriptures as the Word of God. We'll see that God's own perfect integrity guarantees the absolute trustworthiness of the Scriptures. Furthermore, we'll discover how God created the universe through his Word, and how he identifies himself completely with the Word in Jesus Christ. Being the means by which the Holy Spirit creates new life in those who believe, we prove to be disciples by abiding in Jesus' Word. As members of the Church we receive the Word together in community, the same which provides us with the ultimate purpose of the created universe, which is the glorification of Almighty God.

In the next lesson, *The Word that Convicts*, we'll look at how God's Word convicts of sin, righteousness, and judgment. The Word teaches that sin is universal in scope and corrupting in its character. The Word of God also convicts regarding righteousness, revealing God's perfect righteousness and our moral inadequacy. And, it convicts regarding judgment, instructing that God will judge Israel and the nations, the Church, Satan and his angels, and all the wicked dead by his just determination. God's Word also convicts us of the truth--of Jesus Christ, the Kingdom of God, and the integrity of his Word through his messengers, the prophets and the Apostles.

Lesson three, *The Word that Converts*, concentrates on the power of the Word of God to produce new life in the believer. This Word that converts is synonymous with the Gospel of Jesus; it is the good news of salvation which causes us to be "born again," to experience the washing of regeneration, and renewal of the Holy Spirit. The Word produces in we who believe concrete signs of God's renewing power. This same Word that creates new life, sustains us, provides spiritual nourishment, causes our growth, and enables us to defend ourselves against the devil's lies.

Finally, lesson four, *The Word that Calls*, explores the concept of (*metanoia*), that is, repentance towards God, and to faith (*pistis*). Faith in Jesus Christ is the way that

God saves, delivers, and rescues the believer from the penalty, power, and presence of sin. As we turn from sin to God in Christ, the Word leads us to receive God's new nature (regeneration) and become incorporated (adopted) into the people of God (to the *laos* of God) by grace through faith alone. The Word that calls us to salvation also calls us to discipleship (as bondslaves of Jesus), to freedom (as redeemed children) and to mission (to make disciples through our witness and good works).

Truly, the Holy Scriptures are a Word that are profitable for teaching, correction, instruction, and training so that God's person might be completely equipped for any task (2 Tim. 3.16-17). May God bless you as you explore the richness of his God-breathed Word that creates, convicts, converts and calls!

- Rev. Dr. Don L. Davis

Course Requirements

Required Books and Materials

- Bible (for the purposes of this course, your Bible should be a translation [ex. NIV, NASB, RSV, KJV, NKJV, etc.], and not a paraphrase [ex. The Living Bible, The Message]).

- Each Capstone module has assigned textbooks which are read and discussed throughout the course. We encourage you to read, reflect upon, and respond to these with your professors, mentors, and fellow learners. Because of the fluid availability of the texts (e.g., books going out of print), we maintain our *official* Capstone Required Textbook list on our website. Please visit *www.tumi.org/books* to obtain the current listing of this module's texts.

- Paper and pen for taking notes and completing in-class assignments.

Suggested Readings

- Fee, Gordon D. and Douglas Stuart. *How to Read the Bible for All its Worth*. Grand Rapids: Zondervan, 1982.

- Montgomery, J. W. ed. *God's Inerrant Word*. Minneapolis: Bethany, 1974.

- Packer, J. I. *"Fundamentalism" and the Word of God*. London: IVP, 1958.

- Sproul, R. C. *Knowing Scripture*. Downers Grove: IVP, 1977.

Summary of Grade Categories and Weights

Attendance & Class Participation	30%	90 pts
Quizzes	10%	30 pts
Memory Verses	15%	45 pts
Exegetical Project	15%	45 pts
Ministry Project.	10%	30 pts
Readings and Homework Assignments.	10%	30 pts
Final Exam	10%	30 pts
	Total: 100%	300 pts

Grade Requirements

Attendance at each class session is a course requirement. Absences will affect your grade. If an absence cannot be avoided, please let the Mentor know in advance. If you miss a class it is your responsibility to find out the assignments you missed, and to talk with the Mentor about turning in late work. Much of the learning associated with this course takes place through discussion. Therefore, your active involvement will be sought and expected in every class session.

Every class will begin with a short quiz over the basic ideas from the last lesson. The best way to prepare for the quiz is to review the Student Workbook material and class notes taken during the last lesson.

The memorized Word is a central priority for your life and ministry as a believer and leader in the Church of Jesus Christ. There are relatively few verses, but they are significant in their content. Each class session you will be expected to recite (orally or in writing) the assigned verses to your Mentor.

The Scriptures are God's potent instrument to equip the man or woman of God for every work of ministry he calls them to (2 Tim. 3.16-17). In order to complete the requirements for this course you must select a passage and do an inductive Bible study (i.e., an exegetical study) upon it. The study will have to be five pages in length (double-spaced, typed or neatly hand written) and deal with one of the four aspects of the Word of God covered in the four lessons of this course. Our desire and hope is that you will be deeply convinced of Scripture's ability to change and practically affect your life and the lives of those to whom you minister. As you go through the course, be open to finding an extended passage (roughly 4-9 verses) on a subject you would like to study more intensely. The details of the project are covered on pages 10-11, and will be discussed in the introductory session of this course.

Ministry Project

Our expectation is that all students will apply their learning practically in their lives and in their ministry responsibilities. The student will be responsible for developing a ministry project that combines principles learned with practical ministry. The details of this project are covered on page 12, and will be discussed in the introductory session of the course.

Class and Homework Assignments

Classwork and homework of various types may be given during class by your Mentor or be written in your Student Workbook. If you have any question about what is required by these or when they are due, please ask your Mentor.

Readings

It is important that the student read the assigned readings from the text and from the Scriptures in order to be prepared for class discussion. Please turn in the "Reading Completion Sheet" from your Student Workbook on a weekly basis. There will be an option to receive extra credit for extended readings.

Take-Home Final Exam

At the end of the course, your Mentor will give you a final exam (closed book) to be completed at home. You will be asked a question that helps you reflect on what you have learned in the course and how it affects the way you think about or practice ministry. Your Mentor will give you due dates and other information when the Final Exam is handed out.

Grading

The following grades will be given in this class at the end of the session, and placed on each student's record:

A - Superior work   D - Passing work

B - Excellent work   F - Unsatisfactory work

C - Satisfactory work   I - Incomplete

Letter grades with appropriate pluses and minuses will be given for each final grade, and grade points for your grade will be factored into your overall grade point average. Unexcused late work or failure to turn in assignments will affect your grade, so please plan ahead, and communicate conflicts with your instructor.

Exegetical Project

Purpose

As a part of your participation in the Capstone *Conversion and Calling* module of study, you will be required to do an exegesis (inductive study) on one of the following passages in the Word of God:

❏ Psalms 19.7-11

❏ Isaiah 55.8-11

❏ 1 Corinthians 2.9-16

❏ 2 Timothy 3.15-17

❏ 1 Peter 1.22-25

❏ 2 Peter 1.19-21

The purpose of this exegetical project is to give you an opportunity to do a detailed study of a major passage on the nature and function of the Word of God. As you study one of the above texts (or a text which you and your Mentor agree upon which may not be on the list), our hope is that you will be able to show how this passage illumines or makes plain the significance of the Word of God for our spirituality and for our lives together in the Church. We also desire that the Spirit will give you insight as to how you can relate its meaning directly to your own personal walk of discipleship, as well as to the leadership role God has given to you currently in your church and ministry.

Outline and Composition

This is a Bible study project, and, in order to do *exegesis*, you must be committed to understand the meaning of the passage in its own setting. Once you know what it meant, you can then draw out principles that apply to all of us, and then relate those principles to life. A simple three step process can guide you in your personal study of the Bible passage:

1. What was *God saying to the people in the text's original situation*?

2. What principle(s) does *the text teach that is true for all people everywhere*, including today?

3. What is *the Holy Spirit asking me to do with this principle here, today*, in my life and ministry?

Once you have answered these questions in your personal study, you are then ready to write out your insights for your *paper assignment*.

Here is a *sample outline* for your paper:

1. List out what you believe is *the main theme or idea* of the text you selected.

2. *Summarize the meaning* of the passage (you may do this in two or three paragraphs, or, if you prefer, by writing a short verse-by-verse commentary on the passage).

3. *Outline one to three key principles or insights* this text provides on the Word of God.

4. Tell how one, some, or all of the principles may relate to *one or more* of the following:

   a. Your personal spirituality and walk with Christ

   b. Your life and ministry in your local church

   c. Situations or challenges in your community and general society

As an aid or guide, please feel free to read the course texts and/or commentaries, and integrate insights from them into your work. Make sure that you give credit to whom credit is due if you borrow or build upon someone else's insights. Use in-the-text references, footnotes, or endnotes. Any way you choose to cite your references will be acceptable, as long as you 1) use only one way consistently throughout your paper, and 2) indicate where you are using someone else's ideas, and are giving them credit for it. (For more information, see *Documenting Your Work: A Guide to Help You Give Credit Where Credit Is Due* in the Appendix.)

Make certain that your exegetical project, when turned in meets the following standards:

- It is legibly written or typed.

- Is a study of one of the passages above.

- It is turned in on time (not late).

- It is 5 pages in length.

- It follows the outline given above, clearly laid out for the reader to follow.

- It shows how the passage relates to life and ministry today.

Do not let these instructions intimidate you; this is a Bible study project! All you need to show in this paper is that you *studied* the passage, *summarized* its meaning, *drew out* a few key principles from it, and *related* them to your own life and ministry.

Grading   The exegetical project is worth 45 points, and represents 15% of your overall grade, so make certain that you make your project an excellent and informative study of the Word.

Ministry Project

The Word of God is living and active, and penetrates to the very heart of our lives and innermost thoughts (Heb. 4.12). James the Apostle emphasizes the need to be doers of the Word of God, not hearers only, deceiving ourselves. We are exhorted to apply the Word, to obey it. Neglecting this discipline, he suggests, is analogous to a person viewing our natural face in a mirror and then forgetting who we are, and are meant to be. In every case, the doer of the Word of God will be blessed in what he or she does (James 1.22-25).

Our sincere desire is that you will apply your learning practically, correlating your learning with real experiences and needs in your personal life, and in your ministry in and through your church. Therefore, a key part of completing this module will be for you to design a ministry project to help you share some of the insights you have learned from this course with others.

There are many ways that you can fulfill this requirement of your study. You may choose to conduct a brief study of your insights with an individual, or a Sunday School class, youth or adult group or Bible study, or even at some ministry opportunity. What you must do is discuss some of the insights you have learned from class with your audience. (Of course, you may choose to share insights from your Exegetical Project in this module with them.)

Feel free to be flexible in your project. Make it creative and open-ended. At the beginning of the course, you should decide on a context in which you will share your insights, and share that with your instructor. Plan ahead and avoid the last minute rush in selecting and carrying out your project.

After you have carried out your plan, write and turn in to your Mentor a one-page summary or evaluation of your time of sharing. A sample outline of your Ministry Project summary is as follows:

1. Your name

2. The place where you shared, and the audience with whom you shared

3. A brief summary of how your time went, how you felt, and how they responded

4. What you learned from the time

The Ministry Project is worth 30 points and represents 10% of your overall grade, so make certain to share your insights with confidence and make your summary clear.

The Word that Creates

Lesson Objectives

Welcome in the strong name of Jesus Christ! After your reading, study, discussion, and application of the materials in this lesson, you will be able to:

- Defend the idea that the Holy Scriptures are the Word of God, a written record of the Lord's own living and eternal Word.

- Show from Scripture that the God of the Bible, the Triune God, guarantees the truthfulness of the Word of God, which makes it absolutely trustworthy. All things in the universe were made through God's creative and life-giving Word.

- Describe how the Lord God identifies himself completely with the Word of God, especially in Jesus Christ, the Second person of the Trinity, through whom God reveals himself, redeems the world, and will restore the universe under his righteous rule.

- Prove from Scripture that the Word of God, infused as it is with God's very life, is the means by which the Holy Spirit creates new life in those who believe.

- Discuss how continuing in and receiving this implanted Word of God is the true sign of discipleship and authentic adoption into the family of God. As saints of God, we receive the Word of God together in his covenant community.

- Demonstrate how the Word reveals the ultimate purpose of the created universe, which is the glorification of Almighty God.

- Recite from memory a passage relating to the creative power of the Word of God.

Devotion

The Desirability of the Living Word of God

Read Psalm 19.7-11. If our age is known for anything it is the age of passion. People give themselves to acquire things, to experience pleasures, to attain positions, and to accomplish goals, sometimes making great sacrifices for the things that they desire.

Perhaps the saddest tragedy in the lives of millions of people is that they are giving themselves over to things that, in the long run, won't matter at all. They are living for fleeting pleasures, material possessions, and personal accomplishments that within a hundred years either won't exist or won't matter at all. To really live well we must not merely have great passion, but we must direct our passions and desires after the things that will last, and the things that really matter.

According to the Word of God, very few things really matter, and therefore, few things are to be desired and sought after. One of the most significant treasures spoken of in Scripture is the very Word of God itself. God declares that his Word, the written Word of the Holy Scriptures, is a treasure that is worthy of our most sincere and concentrated efforts to acquire. Nothing on earth lasts like it; nothing can provide us with the wisdom, insight, hope, and joy that it gives. The Word of God is a profoundly rich asset, giving light to the eyes, joy to the heart, wisdom to the spirit, and hope to one's life. The psalmist here makes plain the remarkable desirability of the living Word of God to us. There is nothing that we own or could own that is as valuable and important as God's Word regarding his Son, his plan, and our hope. In keeping them we are warned, and in clinging to them there is great reward.

Are you seeking the Word of God like you seek money, or pleasure, or free time, or great opportunity? Nothing in this world is as valuable or as significant as a deep knowledge of God's Word. Where is the desire of your heart today?

After reciting and/or singing the Nicene Creed (located in the Appendix), pray the following prayers:

Nicene Creed and Prayer

> *Eternal God, our Father, we praise you for your desire to reveal yourself to us through your Word. You have blessed us by preserving your gracious promise and pronouncement through the Scriptures, which you inspired by your own Holy Spirit. Now, through that same Spirit, you are teaching us about your Son, and your glorious plan to restore all things in him. How we bless your high and holy name for your living and abiding Word, and we ask that you would grant to us your wisdom as we learn together the power and greatness of your Word.*
>
> *Merciful God, heavenly Father, Thou hast said to us through the mouth of Thy dear Son, our Lord Jesus Christ, "Pray the Lord of the harvest," Upon this Thy divine*

command, we pray from our hearts, that Thou wilt give thy Holy Spirit richly to these Thy servants, together with us and all those who are called to serve Thy word. Amen.

~ Martin Luther. **Devotions and Prayers of Martin Luther**. Trans. Andrew Kosten. Grand Rapids: Baker Book House, 1965. p 77.

Quiz

No quiz this lesson

Scripture Memorization Review

No Scripture memorization this lesson

Assignments Due

No assignments due this lesson

CONTACT

A Question of Expertise

 In general society today it is normal for most people who have professional or personal problems to either handle it on their own, or consult the "experts" - scientists, doctors, counselors, or others who are perceived as the ones who can enable them to overcome their difficulties or solve their problems. What place does the Word of God have today in solving people's problems? In what ways do you see or fail to see a respect for the teaching of the Word of God in society today?

Where Does the Authority Lie?

 Imagine that a critical issue comes up in the youth group of your local church ministry about pre-marital sex. Many of the kids are being taught in their local high schools that sexual activity is normal and expected, and is fine as long as they take precautions against sexually transmitted diseases and the risk of getting pregnant. The arguments being made in high school are becoming somewhat attractive to some of the students in your youth group, who are wondering just how the standards of an ancient book like the Bible relate to them as young people today. What would you say to those kids who are teetering on the brink of rejecting the authority of Scripture for their lives, those who are becoming more and more persuaded that things are okay if we handle them responsibly and openly?

Jesus - Yes; the Bible - No!

There are many people who profess a deep allegiance to the person and teaching of Jesus, but have a problem with the truthfulness of the Bible. Jesus taught love, humility, and good will among people; the Bible, however, is filled with odd teachings about angels, demons, and miracles, things which many modern people find hard or impossible to believe. Do you think it is possible to embrace the person of Jesus Christ while, at the same time, calling certain things of the Bible into question? Can you say "Yes!" to Jesus, but a "No!" or "I'm not sure" to many things in the Scriptures? Must you believe everything that the Bible teaches in order to claim a true relationship and faith in Jesus? Why or why not?

1

The Word that Creates

Segment 1

Rev. Dr. Don L. Davis

The Holy Scriptures are the Word of God, a written record of the Lord's own living and eternal Word. The God of the Bible, the Triune God, guarantees the truthfulness of the Word of God, which makes it absolutely trustworthy. All things in the universe were made through God's creative and life-giving Word. The Lord God identifies himself completely with the Word of God in Jesus Christ, the Second person of the Trinity, through whom God reveals himself, redeems the world, and will restore the universe under his righteous rule.

Summary of Segment 1

Our objective for this first segment of *The Word that Creates* is to enable you to see, comprehend, and understand the implications of how:

- The Holy Scriptures, the living and eternal Word of God, is identified directly with God's person and his work. They are, therefore, completely reliable and absolutely authoritative in all they assert and claim.

- The entire universe and all life it contains was created through the life-giving power of the Word of God.

- God identifies himself completely with the Word of God, especially in the Second person of the Trinity, through whom God reveals himself, redeems the world, and will restore the universe under his righteous rule.

I.   **The Scriptures Are the Word of the Living God, Inspired by His Breath and Associated with His Person and Work.**

A.   The Scriptures are the living and eternal Word that lives and abides forever.

1.   The Word of God is eternal, possessing God's attribute of complete truthfulness and authority, 1 Pet. 1.23-25.

2.   The Scriptures are inspired by the very "breath" of God Almighty.

a.   2 Tim. 3.16-17

b.   God breathed his own creative life into his Word.

3.   We need not believe that God dictated the Scriptures for them to be inspired by him. Rather, we believe that the Holy Spirit used the vocabularies, experiences, and capacities of the authors in the precise way he intended so that the product they produced in their writing was his own creation. The Spirit inspired the writings in such a way that he can be called the author of the documents. It is in this way that the Church has considered the Scriptures to be the authoritative standard and reliable guide for faith and practice.

a.   2 Pet. 1.19-21

b.   Men spoke from God as they were carried along by the Holy Spirit himself.

B. Because they are inspired of God, it is impossible, therefore, for the Scriptures to return void, empty, or fruitless back to him. In every way, God's Word is seen as completely reliable and absolutely authoritative, worthy of our trust and study.

1. Isa. 55.8-11

   a. God's ways are infinitely above our ways, that is, absolutely beyond our searching or discovery.

   b. God's Word is completely effective in all that God ordains and orders it to do.

2. God asserts the absolute certainty of his divine Word, Isa. 44.26-28.

   a. God declares that he will confirm the word of his servant and fulfill the counsel of his messengers. His Word is truth.

   b. God confirms his Word with absolute certainty and faithfulness. As Jesus said in John 10.35, "The Scriptures cannot be broken."

C. Because of its perfect reliability, the Word is everywhere extolled and praised in the Bible.

1. It is praised for its absolute eternality, Matt. 5.18.

2. It is praised through God's exaltation of his Word, Isa. 42.21.

3. It is praised alongside his holy name, Ps. 138.1-2.

4. It is praised for its long lasting reality, Matt. 24.35.

5. The perfection, enlightenment, trustworthiness, and faithfulness of the Word of God is acknowledged and affirmed, Psalms 19 & 119.

II. **God Almighty, Acting through the Creative Force of His Word, Created All Things in the Universe.**

A. The LORD, the God of Israel, is the Creator of the heavens and the earth; the universe is neither self-caused nor self-sustained.

1. Gen. 1.1

2. Prov. 16.4

3. Heb. 1.10

B. Second, God created the universe "*ex nihilo,*" out of, or from nothing.

1. Heb. 11.3

2. Ps. 33.6

3. Ps. 33.8-9

4. 2 Pet. 3.5

C. God created the universe through the Logos, the Word of God, who is Jesus Christ.

1. John 1.1-3

2. Col. 1.16

3. The Word of God has a high place in the creative work of God in the universe-God's Word is a Word that creates!

III. An Intimate Association Exists between God Almighty and His Word, i.e., "The Word."

A. God reveals himself through general revelation. General revelation is that aspect of God revealing himself which is accessible to all persons at all times.

1. God reveals himself generally in the physical order, in the glory of creation and nature, Ps. 19.1.

2. God reveals himself generally in human history: the people of Israel.

3. God reveals himself generally in human nature, Psalm 8.

a. Reason

    b. Conscience

    c. Moral and spiritual qualities

B. God also reveals himself through special revelation. By special revelation we mean God's revealing of himself to particular persons at very specific times and places for his own purposes.

    1. God reveals himself in special revelation through historical events.

        a. The lives of the patriarchs

        b. The Exodus event

        c. The building of the Temple

    2. God reveals himself in special revelation through divine speech.

        a. "The Word of the Lord," whether given audibly, in dreams, or in vision

        b. This mode perfected in the "propositional" Word, the Holy Scriptures

    3. God reveals himself in special revelation through the incarnation of the Word in the person and work of Jesus Christ.

1

a. God identified directly with the Word in the person of Jesus Christ, John 1.1-2.

b. Jesus Christ is the Word of God made flesh, John 1.14.

(1) God revealed concretely in the body, in time and space

(2) A particular revelation for all humankind to see

c. No other person or thing can declare the glory of God like the Word made flesh.

(1) John 1.18

(2) 1 John 1.1-3

d. Jesus' name explicitly called "the Word of God," Rev. 19.13

C. Two significant forms of the Word of God: the propositional Word and the personal Word

1. Form 1: the "propositional" Word of God - the inspired written Word of God

a. The inspired written Word of God, the Hebrew Scriptures of the Old Testament, and the Christian Scriptures of the New Testament

b. A library, inspired by the Spirit over 1500 years, 40 authors

2. Form 2: the "personal" Word of God - the Lord Jesus Christ

a. Jesus is the personal Word of revelation, giving final witness to the person of God, Matt. 11.27.

    b. Jesus is the personal Word of redemption which brings us back to God, John 14.6.

Conclusion

» The Holy Scriptures are the creative Word of God; a written record of the Lord's own living and eternal Word. The Scriptures are absolutely reliable and infallible.

» God created the entire universe through his creative and life-giving Word.

» God identifies himself completely with the Word in the person of Jesus Christ.

Segue 1

Student Questions and Response

Please take as much time as you have available to answer these and other questions that the video brought out concerning the creative power of the Word of God. Be clear and concise in your answers, and where possible, support with Scripture!

1. In what way do the Scriptures assert that they are the Word of God? What does the phrase mean that the Scriptures are inspired by God's very own breath?

2. What is the meaning of the biblical teaching that the Word of God "lives and abides forever?"

3. How might God have inspired the Word of God without merely dictating the Word of God to the authors, or placing them in a trance and taking over their minds? What does the Bible mean when it says that the authors were "carried along" by the Holy Spirit?

4. Why can a believer know that the Scriptures are absolutely trustworthy and reliable?

5. What are the implications of: the Word of God is everywhere extolled and praised throughout Scripture?

6. What is the relationship between the creation of the universe and the Word of God? What is the meaning of the Latin phrase, "*ex nihilo*," and how does this concept relate to God's topic of creation?

7. What does Scripture say about the relationship of God's creation of the universe and the Logos, or the Word of God (i.e., Jesus Christ)?

8. What is the meaning of "general revelation?" What are the specific ways God has revealed himself generally to all humankind?

9. What is the meaning of the phrase "special revelation?" What are the specific ways in which God has revealed himself to particular people at specific times and places?

10. What is the difference between the "propositional" and "personal" Word of God? How are they related? Does one take precedence (i.e., is it more important) than the other? Explain.

The Word that Creates

Segment 2

Rev. Dr. Don L. Davis

The Word of God is the means by which the Holy Spirit creates new life in those who believe. Therefore, continuing in and receiving this implanted Word of God is the true sign of discipleship and authentic adoption into the family of God. As saints of God, we receive the Word of God together in his covenant community. Finally, because of the trustworthiness of the Word, it alone can declare to us the ultimate purpose of the created universe, which is the glorification of Almighty God.

Our objective for this second segment of *The Word that Creates* is to enable you to see that:

- God's Word is infused with God's very life, and therefore, no spirituality or authentic religion is possible without the life-giving power of the Word of God. God creates new life in believers through his Word, enlightened by the Holy Spirit.

Summary of Segment 2

- The true sign of discipleship is to abide in and continue in the ongoing reception of the Word of God as spirit and truth. Spiritual maturity is directly connected to hearing and obeying God's Word in the Church.

- Because of its infallible authority, only the Word of God can provide us with the ultimate purpose for the created universe, which is to bring God honor and glory in all things.

Video Segment 2 Outline

I. **The Word of God Is Infused with God's Own Life, and Therefore Creates New Life in Those Who Believe.**

A. The Word creates spiritual life in response to belief in the work of Jesus Christ.

    1. The Word of God is absolutely primary in creating new spiritual life in the believer.

        a. James 1.18

        b. James 1.21

    2. The Word of God is the instrument, the imperishable seed, that births new life in us through our faith in Jesus Christ, 1 Pet. 1.22-23.

    3. The Gospel concerning Jesus and his Kingdom is not of human origin, but "is itself the very Word of God," 1 Thess. 2.13.

B. Spiritual life is created by the living Word of God: we live by every word which proceeds from the mouth of God.

1. We hold this view on the authority of Jesus Christ.

    a. The temptation of Jesus

    b. The quotation of Deuteronomy: the singular role of the Word of God, Deut. 8.3, cf. Matt. 4.4

2. The Word of God has remarkable spiritual vitality and creative power to spiritually enlighten the soul, Ps. 19.7-11.

3. No part of the Word of God is to be considered useless or superfluous; every jot and tittle will be fulfilled, and none of it shall pass away.

4. God absolutely refuses to break his covenant promise: the Scriptures are reliable because God is faithful.

    a. 2 Kings 13.23

    b. 1 Chron. 16.14-17

C. God provides understanding for his Word through the sending of his Holy Spirit to believers, 1 Cor. 2.9-16.

    1. The unbeliever (i.e., "natural man") does not have the Holy Spirit, and therefore cannot understand the Word's message or teaching.

2. The spiritual person, (i.e., the one who has and is led by the Holy Spirit), not only understands what the Word of God says, but escapes the judgment of those who fail to comprehend it.

3. The same Spirit who inspired the Word is the one who interprets it, 2 Pet. 1.21.

II. The True Sign of Discipleship Is to Continue in and Abide in the Word of God as Nourishment.

A. The sign of true discipleship is to continue in and abide in the Word of Christ.

1. John 8.31-32

2. "Abide" is to remain present, to make one's home in, to dwell in, Ps. 1.1-3.

3. The sense of abiding is similar to the OT notion of meditation.

a. Ps. 1.1-3

b. Josh. 1.8

B. Spiritual growth and maturity are dependent on feeding upon the truths in the creative and life-giving Word of God.

1.   Believers are to desire the pure milk of the Word of God in order that we might be able to grow as we feed upon it, 1 Pet. 2.2.

2.   Paul, in his challenge to the elders of Ephesus, commended them to God and the Word of his grace "which is able to build you up and to give you the inheritance among all those who are sanctified," Acts 20.32.

3.   The Colossians are exhorted to let the Word of God dwell richly in them, Col. 3.16.

4.   Paul gives Timothy authoritative charge to study to show himself a workman to God approved as he rightly divided (dissected) the Word of truth, 2 Tim. 2.15.

5.   There are many ways to abide in the Word of God.

   a.   We are to *read* it. Revelation 1.3 promises a blessing to those who read the Word of God.

   b.   We are to *memorize* it. In Psalm 19.11 David says he hides God's Word in his heart that he might not sin against the Lord.

   c.   We are to *meditate* upon it. Psalm 1.3 says that the godly man meditates, murmurs and chews on the Word of God day and night.

   d.   We are to *study* it. The Bereans are called "more noble" than the Thessalonicans in Acts 17.11 because they not only heard the words of the Apostle Paul, but studied the Scriptures daily to validate Paul's Gospel.

e. We are to *hear it preached and taught* in the Church. We are not to despise prophesies, but hear the Word for, as Romans 10.17 suggests, "faith comes by hearing, and hearing by the Word of God."

  f. We are to *include it in all our living and conversation*. The Word that creates must become the dominant force in our lives as spoken in the words of the Shema, Deut. 6.4-9.

C. This creative Word of God must be heard and obeyed in the context of Christian community.

  1. Do not despise prophesying, nor to quench the Holy Spirit, 1 Thess. 5.19-22.

  2. The Word will come in the midst of the assembly, 1 Cor. 14.26.

  3. God has given to the Church men and women specially endowed by the Holy Spirit to teach the Word of God, Eph. 4.11-13.

III. The Word Reveals God's Eternal Purpose for the Universe: That All Things Might Bring Glory and Honor to Him as Lord.

A. One underlying pulse of energy throbs from the heart of the Divine Story. All things were created to bring glory, honor, and praise to himself and his glorious Name.

  1. All things were created for God's designed purpose, Prov. 16.4.

2. All things in heaven and in earth, whether visible or invisible, all angels, creatures, whether human or animal, and all that exist were created by God and for his glory.

   a. Col. 1.16

   b. Rev. 4.11

   c. Ps. 150.6

3. The nation of Israel, God's chosen people, were selected for his ultimate glory.

   a. Isa. 43.7

   b. Isa. 43.21

   c. Cf. Isa. 43.25; 60.1, 3, 21

4. God saves humankind in order to bring glory and honor to himself, Rom. 9.23; Eph. 2.7.

5. All the service and the works that God's people accomplish are to be done for God's ultimate glory, 1 Cor. 10.31; John 15.8; Matt. 5.16.

6. Believer's high purpose: personal witness to the glory of God in Christ, and sharing in that same glory at his appearing.

Taken as a whole, the Bible differs in its subject and purpose from any other book in the world. It stands supreme as reflecting the place of [humankind] and [its] opportunity of salvation, the supreme character and work of Jesus Christ as the only Savior, and gives in detail the infinite glories that belong to God himself. It is the one book that reveals the Creator to the creature and discloses the plan by which all [humankind] in all [its] imperfections can be reconciled in eternal fellowship with the eternal God.
~ Lewis Sperry Chafer. *Major Bible Themes.* Grand Rapids: Zondervan, 1974. p. 29.

a. John 17.22

b. Col. 3.4

B. When we submit to God's creative Word, it provides us with strength and direction in order to accomplish this purpose of honoring and glorifying him.

1. It discloses our inner motives and desires, Heb. 4.12.

2. It aligns our wavering hearts with the majesty of God's eternal purpose.

   a. Scripture as the joy and rejoicing of our hearts, Jer. 15.16

   b. The Word of God causes great movement deep inside our hearts as we yield to its power, Jer. 20.9.

3. It transforms us by the renewing of our minds to the perfect will of God, Rom. 12.1-2.

Conclusion

» The Word of God is infused with God's own life and is the means by which the Holy Spirit creates new life in those who believe.

» True disciples of Jesus Christ abide in this implanted Word.

» The Holy Spirit teaches us that the ultimate purpose of the created universe is to glorify Almighty God.

» The Scriptures, the Word that creates, enable us through the Spirit to glorify God as we live under God's rule.

The following questions were designed to help you review the material in the second video segment which focused on the life-giving properties of the Word of God in our lives. Be clear and concise in your answers, and where possible, support with Scripture!

1. How does the Bible describe the role that the Scriptures play in providing new life to the one who believes in Christ? What role does faith play together with the Word to create the new birth?

2. In what way does Jesus' temptation teach us of the power of the Word of God for our lives? What truth did Jesus cite when confronted with the devil and his deceptions in the wilderness?

3. What role does the Holy Spirit play in helping the spiritual person grasp the meaning of the Holy Scriptures? What about the natural person--can they understand them? Why or why not?

4. What is the true sign of discipleship in Jesus Christ? Describe the relationship between spiritual growth and feeding upon the Word of God?

5. What are some of the ways that Scripture suggests that one can abide in the Word of God? How does abiding in the Word connect to living in Christian community?

6. What particular people has God given to the Church to help it understand and apply the Word of God? What is their role in helping equip Christians to do ministry?

7. According to Scripture, what is God's eternal purpose for the created universe?

8. Ultimately, what is the high purpose that God has appointed for believers, and how are they to carry that purpose out in their lives?

9. In what way are the Scriptures unique and supremely above all other books in the world?

10. What can we expect to occur in our hearts and our lives when we submit to God's creative Word? Explain.

CONNECTION

Summary of Key Concepts

This lesson highlights certain critical aspects of the creative power of the Word of God, objectively in the creation of the universe, and subjectively, in the creation of new spiritual life in the heart of the believer. In every sense, the notion of the Word of God is significant for understanding God's work in the world, and throughout human history.

- The Holy Scriptures are the living and eternal Word of God. They are infused with God's very own life through his inspiration of them, as well as identified directly with God's person and his work.

- Because the Scriptures are so intimately associated with God's person and work, they are therefore completely reliable and absolutely authoritative for all matters of faith in everything they assert and claim to be true.

- The entire universe and all life it contains was created "*ex nihilo*" (i.e., out of nothing) by the life-giving power of the Word of God, that is, by the words he spoke at the time of creation. In addition, God Almighty created all things through the Living Word, Jesus Christ (John 1.1-3; Col. 1.16).

- The Scriptures are the "propositional" Word of God, inspired by the Spirit, and includes both the Old Testament (i.e., the Hebrew Scriptures) and the New Testament (i.e., the Christian Scriptures).

- God identifies himself completely with the personal Word of God in Jesus Christ, through whom God reveals himself, redeems the world, and will restore the universe under his righteous rule.

- The Word of God, being authored by the Holy Spirit and therefore infused with God's own life, is the critical instrument by which new life is created in those who believe in Jesus. The message of the Gospel is the spiritual seed that causes us to be born from above.

- The authentic sign of true discipleship in Christ is abiding in and continuing in the Word of Jesus, which liberates and sets believers free.

- God has granted to every believer the Holy Spirit in order that we might understand and grasp the meaning of the Scriptures that he inspired (1 Cor. 2.9-16 cf. 2 Pet. 1.21-22).

- The Holy Spirit teaches us that the ultimate purpose of the created universe is to glorify Almighty God (Isa. 43.7; Prov. 16.4; 1 Cor. 10.31).

- The Scriptures, the Word that creates, enable us through the Spirit to glorify God as we live under God's rule.

1

Now is the time for you to discuss with your fellow students your questions about the power of the Word that creates. What particular questions do you have in light of the material you have just studied? Perhaps the questions below might spark your discussion together, and help you form your own, more specific and critical questions.

* When we say that the Scriptures are inspired by God, do we mean the "original autographs" (i.e., the documents that prophets and Apostles wrote), the translations, copies of the translations, or everything?

* What impact on discussions about evolution does our belief that God created the world through his Word have? Is evolutionary theory something we need to be concerned about or not?

* If the Word of God is living and active and creative, why doesn't it seem to work the same way in every person's heart that hears it? Why do so many people reject the message of the Word today?

* What exactly is the relationship between the Word of God in Jesus and the Word of God in Scripture? Which one is to take precedence over the other; are they meant to be taken and revered in the same way?

* How are we to relate to the Holy Spirit, practically speaking, so we can know that he will teach us as we study the Word of God?

* If I am to study the Word of God in the context of community, what is the role and importance of my personal study of the Word of God? What if I disagree with some of the things that are being taught in my church, or by my pastor-what am I to do then?

CASE STUDIES

A Serious Case of Disagreement

As a church has been going through a series of teachings on the Second Coming of Christ, a young Christian leader has encountered teachings in the pastor's sermons that she doesn't understand, and, on first glance, does not agree with. She has spent some time discussing with the pastor some of the points, and none of them are critical, in the sense that they deny anything taught in the Scriptures. The pastor has made it plain that these are merely his opinions about the Scriptures, but is a strong teacher and many are finding his ideas convincing. The pastor is a biblical leader, a fine Christian teacher, and a humble brother in Christ. What ought the sister to do in this situation?

A Denial of the Faith?

2 In a science class at school, one of the students in the youth group is having to write a term paper on the theory of evolution. This same student has been learning at church how God created the worlds through the Word of God, and even more specifically, through Jesus Christ. He believes the Scriptures, that the Bible's teaching on creation is correct, and yet the Bible does not appear to address all of the issues that he is encountering in class about science. He does not want to turn his science class into a religious discussion group, but he is struggling with finding a way to talk about the Bible's view of creation in his high school science class. If this young brother came to you for advice, what would you counsel him to do or not do?

God's Word according to King James of England

3 Serious disagreement and conflict has arisen in one of the church's home Bible studies over which translations are okay to be used. One faction of older believers has asserted that the only Bible we should use in the group is the King James Bible, a tried and true translation that has long been revered and treasured in the church. A group of younger folk are insistent on using some of the "modern" translations, because they find them so much easier to study and memorize. To those of the older faction, when verses are read from the newer translation, it is as if the entire meaning of the verse has changed. Both sides know that the Bible was not written originally in English, but no one in either faction understands Hebrew or Greek. As pastor, how would you resolve this dilemma in the home group?

You Need the Holy Spirit

4 After hearing a teaching on television that said no one can understand the Bible without the aid of the Holy Spirit, one of the deacons at church is deeply concerned about his own lack of understanding of the Bible. While he understands that the Holy Spirit has indwelt and sealed him once he believed (e.g., Rom. 8.1-18; Eph. 1.13; Gal. 5.16-23), he doesn't know what it means to be "taught" by the Holy Spirit. He is deeply skeptical of going through a lot of emotional exercises in order to say that he is being taught by the Spirit, and everyone recognizes this dear brother to be a mature, godly, and Christlike servant in the church. Still, he wants to understand what it means to be taught by the Spirit. How would you instruct this brother to understand the role of the Holy Spirit's teaching ministry in his ongoing understanding of the Bible?

1

The Holy Scriptures are the Word of God, a written record of the Lord's own living and eternal Word. Because they are inspired by the Holy Spirit (literally, God-breathed) they are absolutely trustworthy and reliable in all they assert and claim. The Word of God provides us with God's eternal purpose for creation, that is, that all things were made through God's creative and life-giving Word for his ultimate glory. The Lord God identifies himself completely with the Word of God in Jesus Christ. He is the One through whom God reveals himself, redeems the world, and will restore the universe under his righteous rule. This Word by the Spirit creates new life in those who believe. True discipleship is abiding in this Word in the Church, which produces in the believer spiritual maturity, depth, and growth in God's purpose and will.

Restatement of the Lesson's Thesis

1

If you are interested in pursuing some of the ideas of *The Word that Creates*, you might want to give these books a try:

Resources and Bibliographies

Fee, Gordon D. and Douglas Stuart. *How to Read the Bible for All its Worth*. Grand Rapids: Zondervan, 1982.

Montgomery, John Warwick. *God's Inerrant Word*. Minneapolis: Bethany Fellowship, 1973.

Sproul, R.C. *Knowing Scripture*. Downers Grove: InterVarsity, 1977.

Tenney, Merrill. *The Bible: The Living Word of Revelation*. Grand Rapids: Zondervan, 1968.

Now is the time to try to nail down your study of the creative power of the Word of God to a very real practical ministry connection that you are facing or have faced; one which you will think about and pray for throughout this next week. How in particular does the creative power of the Word of God need to be demonstrated in your life and ministry this week? Have you gained some insights in this lesson that need to be emphasized in what you are doing in your ministry at church? What particular concept has the Holy Spirit suggested that you need to understand better, or something you ought to take up to study more thoroughly? Meditate in the presence of the Lord for a moment and ask him to reveal to you specifically how you can make more plain the reality that his Word is a Word that creates in your church, your family and your life.

Ministry Connections

Counseling and Prayer

Ask God the Holy Spirit to illumine your heart regarding the life-giving power and divine energy which animates and fills the Word of God. Ask God to give you greater insight into the meaning of the Word of God, and to give you more and better time to spend reading, studying, memorizing and meditating on the Word in your life during the week. Pray too that God would make the sermons and teachings from your church come alive for you as you listen and meditate on these truths. Above all, ask God to use you more and more as a Spirit-taught teacher of the Word of God to make the person and purpose of God more plain through your teaching. The better you understand the Word of God, the more it seeps into your own soul and mind and influences you, the greater the impact your ministry and witness will have, both in your church and through the various responsibilities God has given you to represent him.

ASSIGNMENTS

Scripture Memory

2 Peter 1.19-21

Reading Assignment

To prepare for class, please visit *www.tumi.org/books* to find next week's reading assignment, or ask your mentor.

Other Assignments

You will be quizzed on the content (the video content) of this lesson next week. Make sure that you spend time covering your notes, especially focusing on the main ideas of the lesson. Read the assigned reading, and summarize each reading with no more than a paragraph or two for each. In this summary please give your best understanding of what you think was the main point in each of the readings. Do not be overly concerned about giving detail; simply write out what you consider to be the main point discussed in that section of the book. Please bring these summaries to class next week. (Please see the "Reading Completion Sheet" at the end of this lesson.)

In next week's lesson we will continue to explore the power of the Word of God as an instrument of the Holy Spirit to convict the world of sin, righteousness, and judgment. Regarding sin, the Word convicts us of our disobedience to God's law and our disobedience. Regarding righteousness, it reveals the Lord as infinitely righteous and our own righteousness as unacceptable. Regarding judgment, it shows God's intention to bring to account all beings in conjunction to his righteous demands, and their obedience to them. We'll also see how the Word convicts us of the truth of Jesus Christ as the Bible's central theme and focus, the Kingdom of God as the backdrop for God's story, the prophets and Apostles as true and reliable witnesses of God's revelation in the world.

Looking Forward to the Next Lesson

1

Name _____

Date _____

For each assigned reading, write a brief summary (one or two paragraphs) of the author's main point. (For additional readings, use the back of this sheet.)

Reading 1

Title and Author: _____ Pages _____

Reading 2

Title and Author: _____ Pages _____

LESSON
2

The Word that Convicts

Lesson Objectives

Welcome in the strong name of Jesus Christ! After your reading, study, discussion, and application of the materials in this lesson, you will be able to articulate and defend with Scripture the truth that:

- The Word of God is that Word that convicts of sin, righteousness, and judgment.

- Of all the ways we can understand the person and works of God, it is the Word of God in Scripture that enables us to understand sin - that it is universal in scope and corrupting in its character.

- God's Law convicts us of our sin, revealing the distance between our actions and intentions and God's holy demands.

- The Word of God convicts regarding righteousness, revealing our inadequacy in keeping God's Law, and revealing God's righteousness by faith through the death and resurrection of Jesus Christ.

- The Word of God convicts regarding judgment, revealing God's intent to bring to account all creatures everywhere, and his upcoming judgment on Israel and the nations, the Church, on Satan and his angels, and all the wicked dead.

- The Word of God produces conviction regarding the nature of truth, i.e., what is true concerning God, his work in the world, and the destiny and purpose of humankind.

- The Word of God also produces conviction about the primary subject of the Scriptures: the revelation of the person and work of Jesus Christ.

- God's Word also produces conviction regarding the overarching backdrop of all of God's revelation: the revelation of his kingdom plan.

- God's Word produces conviction through the integrity of God's chosen messengers, the prophets and the Apostles, who were given the task to represent and to speak of God's person and plan.

The Blessing of Misery

Read Psalm 32.1-11. Have you ever struggled with a guilty conscience? Not of false guilt, mind you, but knowing in your heart you did something wrong, and you were feeling bad about what you did-you wanted to make up for it, resolve it, do right by the person you hurt? This sense is one of the healthiest inner states you can ever be in. While it may appear miserable and difficult, even shameful, the sense of being convicted of your wrong, and what you did, is one of the most significant feelings to have. No doubt about it; this state of being convicted, of sensing your own guilt before God in your conscience, is associated with feelings. In a real sense, the person who does wrong and has no sense, no feeling of responsibility or blame within, is in serious spiritual trouble. To lack the ability to be convicted by God makes you vulnerable to do wrong with no sense of repentance, sorrow, or willingness to change. David in this psalm speaks directly of God's ability to forgive, and his own sense of pain and shame while he delayed his repentance and return to the Lord. The misery we sense when the Holy Spirit convicts us of our sin is a blessed kind of misery, different than all other forms of inner struggle or pain. This misery can enable us to understand our own transgression, God's righteous standard, our inability to keep God's truth in our own strength, and our indebtedness to God for the wrong we've done. This misery leads us to the truth about ourselves and about God; we will be miserable until we admit our guilt before God; this misery leads us to the only one who can forgive us for our sin. Of all the things we need if we are to remain intimate with God, the greatest is a conscience that can be easily made aware of what God wants and his willingness to show us mercy if we are only ready to admit what we have done wrong, and come to him to receive his mercy afresh. Thank God for the blessing of misery!

After reciting and/or singing the Nicene Creed (located in the Appendix), pray the following prayers:

> *Eternal God, our Father, thank you for the life-giving power of the Word of God, and how your Holy Spirit implants that Word within our hearts. Thank you for his gentle convicting power, that reveals to us both our unworthiness as well as your great mercy. You are willing to forgive those who come broken and open before you. Give us grace today to stand in need of the convicting power of your Word, and the cleansing power of your Son's blood. With you and you alone there is mercy and forgiveness and grace. To you be the glory, in Jesus' precious name, Amen!*

Lord God, heavenly Father, from whom we continuously receive all good things so lavishly, and by whom we are daily safe-guarded from all evil so graciously, help us, we beseech Thee, to appropriate all these gifts through Thy Holy Spirit with full heart and true faith, so that we may thank and praise Thy gentle goodness and mercy; through Jesus Christ Thy Son our Lord. Amen.

~ Martin Luther. **Devotions and Prayers of Martin Luther.** Trans. Andrew Kosten. Grand Rapids: Baker Book House, 1965. p 77.

Quiz

Put away your notes, gather up your thoughts and reflections, and take the quiz for Lesson 1, *The Word that Creates.*

Scripture Memorization Review

Review with a partner, write out and/or recite the text for last class session's assigned memory verse: 2 Peter 1.19-21.

Assignments Due

Turn in your summary of the reading assignment for last week, that is, your brief response and explanation of the main points that the authors were seeking to make in the assigned reading (Reading Completion Sheet).

CONTACT

Will the True Religion Please Stand Up?

 In a philosophy class at the local junior college, one of the church elders encountered the idea of "cultural relativism." This idea suggests that all cultures are equal, and all of their various belief systems, religious notions, and ethical norms are equally valid. This idea has troubled the church leader, who believes that Jesus Christ is somehow unique and primary above and beyond all other religious systems and ideas. How ought he to understand this particular view of "cultural relativism," and how does this idea relate to the Bible's claim that God's revelation in Jesus is somehow once-for-all and final (cf. Heb. 1.1-2)?

Which Songs Are Really the "Songs of Zion"?

A serious debate is brewing among the members of the youth group regarding what kind of music is acceptable for young Christians to listen to. It all started when one of the teens brought one of their favorite rap artists in to play in the CD player at youth group, and some of the kids objected to the kinds of things the artist was referring to. The teen who brought the music, a growing Christian who loves God much, was hurt by the controversy, believing that it is important to understand what is going on in the world if he is to be a good witness to his lost friends. Others, equally in love with God, argue that this kind of music is not godly; all of the talk about violence and pain and struggle is not encouraging but depressing to them. Both sides appear to be equally convinced of the importance of the issue and the truth of their particular "side." What is the best way to resolve this struggle, this impasse between these opposing parties on this issue of music?

It Just Isn't Fair!

Recently, a small group studying the Last Things and the Second Coming began to study the various judgments associated with the end times. For one of the sisters in the group, the study has caused much internal strain and confusion, especially on one point-the idea of God judging those who have never heard about Christ. In her mind, the idea that God will judge all people, even those who have not had the chance to hear about Jesus and his love, is offensive. "God can't do that-that wouldn't be fair to blame those who, due to no fault of their own, never come to know God. They will wind up being judged by God and even going to hell simply because nobody ever told them about the Lord." For others in the study, the issue isn't God's fairness but God's holiness. They argue that if God does not judge all according to the standard he has set down (i.e., faith in Christ) he would violate his own integrity, for he has said that the one who calls on the name of the Lord will be saved (cf. Rom. 10.9-10). While they continue to discuss it openly, they haven't come any closer to resolving the issue. What should they do?

CONTENT ▸ **The Word that Convicts**

Segment 1

Rev. Dr. Don L. Davis

Summary of Segment 1

In this segment, we will explore how the Word of God, as an instrument of the Holy Spirit, convicts the world of sin, righteousness, and judgment. In regards to sin, the Word of God convicts us of our disobedience to God's law and failure to align our lives with his holy character and demands. In regards to righteousness, the Word of God reveals the distance between the Lord as an infinitely righteous God and our own righteousness, which is unacceptable to him. Finally, we will look at the Word of God in regards to its teaching on judgment, and learn of God's intent to bring to account all beings in conjunction to his righteous demands, and their obedience to them.

Our objective for this first segment of *The Word that Convicts* is to enable you to see that:

- The Word of God is that Word that convicts of sin, righteousness, and judgment.

- Of all the ways we can understand the person and works of God, it is the Word of God in Scripture that enables us to understand sin, that it is universal in scope and corrupting in its character.

- God's Law convicts us of our sin, revealing the distance between our actions and intentions and God's holy demands.

- The Word of God convicts regarding righteousness, revealing our inadequacy in keeping God's Law, and revealing God's righteousness by faith through the death and resurrection of Jesus Christ.

- The Word of God convicts regarding judgment, revealing God's intent to bring to account all creatures everywhere, and his upcoming judgment on Israel and the nations, the Church, on Satan and his angels, and all the wicked dead.

I. The Holy Spirit, through the Word of God, Convicts the World of Sin.

A. The Scriptures teach that sin is universal in scope and corrupting in its nature.

   1. Sin is universal in scope.

      a. Romans 3.23 says that all have sinned and fall short of God's glorious design.

      b. Sin is against God and sin is disobedience against his commandments.

         (1) Ps. 51.4

         (2) Luke 15.18

   2. Sin is everything that is contrary to and fails to conform to God's character and purpose.

      a. It touches all people and corrupts all humankind equally.

      b. Sin is universal in scope, utterly corrupting character, Rom. 3.9-12.

   3. We are guilty before God, Rom. 5.18-19.

      a. On the basis of our own sinful acts

Video Segment 1
Outline

John 16.7-11
"Nevertheless, I tell you the truth: it is to your advantage that I go away, for if I do not go away, the Helper will not come to you. But if I go, I will send him to you. And when he comes, he will convict the world concerning sin and righteousness and judgment: concerning sin, because they do not believe in me; concerning righteousness, because I go to the Father, and you will see me no longer; concerning judgment, because the ruler of this world is judged."

b. Through our intimate association with Adam's sin (cf. Rom. 5.18-19)

B. We are convicted of sin through the condemnation of God's Law.

    1. God's Law is holy, good, and acceptable, and represents his demands on us as his creatures; it reveals our own sinfulness.

      a. Rom. 7.7-8

      b. Rom. 7.12

    2. Due to the weakness of our flesh, no one can be saved by their efforts at keeping the works of the Law.

      a. None of us has ever kept God's Law in a way that is acceptable to him, Gal. 3.10-12.

      b. The Law is a closed system. Not to obey God's Law in even the smallest measure is to become guilty of it all, James 2.10-11.

C. The Word of God convicts and produces broken godly remorse, opening up the hearer to God's gospel truth.

    1. The Word of God has spiritual power to protect us from sin, Ps. 119.11.

2

2. God's Word produced conviction in the remnant after the Captivity, leading them to glorify God in their sacrifices and obedience, Ezra 7.10ff.

3. God's Word produced conviction of sin in the great revival of Josiah which revived the nation, 2 Kings 22.13.

II. The Holy Spirit, through the Word of God, Convicts the World of Righteousness.

A. The Word of God reveals four aspects of righteousness.

1. God Almighty is perfectly righteous in his being. His righteousness is revealed to be unchangeable and infinite.

   a. God's righteous being never wavers or changes, James 1.17.

   b. God is righteous in everything he does, Deut. 32.4.

2. The righteousness of humankind is seen as both stained and unacceptable to God, Isa. 64.6-7.

3. The third aspect of biblical righteousness is the kind that God lays to our account because we believe in Jesus Christ.

   a. Rom. 3.21-23

   b. 2 Cor. 5.21

4. The final aspect concerns the indwelling Holy Spirit who produces righteousness in us as we yield to him in trust and obedience, Rom. 8.3-4.

B. Scripture allows no person to take pride in their own righteousness.

1. All humanity is convicted as unrighteous before God, Rom. 3.19.

2. Without Jesus Christ, none are acceptable to God; all are lost, condemned, and utterly doomed to experience God's wrath and displeasure, John 3.36.

III. The Holy Spirit, through the Word of God, Convicts the World of Judgment.

A. All unbelievers are condemned and subject to God's wrath according to Scripture.

1. Unbelievers are called the "children of wrath," Eph. 2.1-3.

2. God has appointed a day to judge the world through Jesus Christ, Acts 17.30-31.

B. God will judge all people everywhere on the basis of what they have done, whether good or evil.

1. Jesus declares in Revelation 22.12 that he soon will return to judge all people according to the deeds they have done.

2. 1 Kings 8.39 - "Render to each whose heart you know, according to all his ways (for you, you only, know the hearts of all the children of mankind)."

3. Job 34.11 - "For according to the work of a man he will repay him, and according to his ways he will make it befall him."

4. Ps. 62.12 - "For you will render to a man according to his work."

5. Prov. 24.12 - "Will he not repay man according to his work?"

6. Isa. 40.10 - "Behold, the Lord God comes with might, and his arm rules for him; behold, his reward is with him, and his recompense before him."

7. Jer. 17.10 - "I the Lord search the heart and test the mind, to give every man according to his ways, according to the fruit of his deeds."

8. Jer. 32.19 - "Great in counsel and mighty in deed, whose eyes are open to all the ways of the children of man, rewarding each one according to his ways and according to the fruit of his deeds."

9. Ezek. 18.30 - "Therefore I will judge you, O house of Israel, every one according to his ways, declares the Lord God."

10. Col. 3.23-25 - "For the wrongdoer will be paid back for the wrong he has done, and there is no partiality."

C. God's judgment will be both rigorous and universal: God Almighty will hold all beings accountable for their responses to his holy will.

1. God will judge Israel and the nations, Rom. 10 & 11.

2. God will judge the Church, 1 Pet. 4.17.

3. God will judge Satan and the fallen angels, Rev. 20.10.

4. God will judge the wicked dead, Rev. 20.11-15.

Conclusion

» The Word of God, as an instrument of the Holy Spirit, convicts the world of sin, righteousness, and judgment.

» In regards to sin, the Word of God convicts us of our disobedience to God's Law and failure to align our lives with his holy character and demands.

» In regards to righteousness, the Word of God reveals the distance between the Lord as an infinitely righteous God and our own righteousness, which is unacceptable to him.

Please take as much time as you have available to answer these and other questions that the video brought out about the Word of God's ability to convict of sin, righteousness, and judgment. Be clear and concise in your answers, and where possible, support with Scripture!

1. How are we to understand the relationship between the Holy Spirit and the Holy Scriptures? Is it valid to say that the Spirit's ministry operates, among other ways, through the Word of God, which is inspired by God's very own breath?

2. In what ways do the Scriptures convict the world of sin? How are we to understand sin as a concept in the Old Testament? What about this same concept through the New Testament?

3. Describe the four aspects of righteousness discussed in the Scriptures? Why is it critical to understand these different aspects when speaking of the Word of God's ability to convict the world of righteousness?

4. In what way does God's righteousness become our own, imputed (given) to us by God himself?

5. How does the Word of God describe God's intention to judge humankind? On what basis will God judge all people everywhere, according to the Scriptures?

6. List some of the groups and entities God intends on bringing ultimately to judgment? What do we learn about God through Scripture's teaching regarding his intent to judge all the world?

7. How does the Word of God actually convict the world of judgment? What is the relationship between God's judgments in the world and the Gospel of Jesus Christ?

Segue 1

Student Questions and Response

The Word that Convicts

Segment 2

Rev. Dr. Don L. Davis

Summary of Segment 2

In this segment we will discover the Word of God's ability to convict regarding the nature of truth, and therefore learn of its capacity to transform our lives and perspectives through the Holy Spirit. The Word of God reveals the Christ-centered nature of God's revelation, the Kingdom Story as the backdrop of God's overall teaching throughout Scripture, and the integrity of the Bible because of its association with the Holy Spirit through the inspired prophets and Apostles. Their testimony provides the Scriptures with final authority for faith and practice, and utter reliability in matters of judgment and truth.

Our objective for this second segment of *The Word that Convicts* is to enable you to understand and articulate to others the truths that:

- The Word of God convicts us of the truth. God's Word is inspired by the Holy Spirit and connected with the God of truth who cannot lie. It is, therefore, God's unfailing witness and record of the truth. It produces conviction regarding the nature of truth, i.e., what is true concerning God, his work in the world, and the destiny and purpose of humankind.

- God's Word produces deep conviction about the primary subject of the Scriptures: the revelation of the person and work of Jesus Christ.

- God's Word also produces conviction regarding the overarching backdrop of all of God's revelation: the revelation of his kingdom plan.

- God has established his Word. It produces conviction through the integrity of God's chosen messengers, the prophets and Apostles, who were given the task to represent and to speak of God's person and plan.

I.   God's Word Convicts Us about the Truth through its Primary Subject: the Person and Work of Jesus Christ.

Video Segment 2
Outline

    A. The master theme of Scripture is Jesus Christ. *A knowledge of Jesus is the most important hermeneutic key to interpreting the Bible.*

        1. On the Emmaus Road, Jesus declared himself as the key to interpreting the Scriptures to the two travelers, Luke 24.25-27.

John 17.17-19
Sanctify them in the truth; your word is truth. As you sent me into the world, so I have sent them into the world. And for their sake I consecrate myself, that they also may be sanctified in truth.

        2. After his resurrection, Jesus taught his Apostles how he was the Bible's interpretive center because of his suffering, death and resurrection, Luke 24.44-48.

        3. Jesus rebuked the Pharisees for their mishandling of Scripture as they studied it with great diligence yet missed him as its central topic and theme, John 5.39-40.

        4. The writer of the Hebrews refers to a quote from God's anointed who recognizes how God's book speaks about him, Heb. 10.5-7.

        5. Finally, Jesus affirms in the Sermon on the Mount that he did not come to abolish the Law and the Prophets but to fulfill them, Matt. 5.17.

    B. Scripture portrays Jesus Christ as the Bible's topical and thematic center.

        1. Jesus is the Final Exegete of Scripture in his interpretation of the Old Testament, (cf. the Sermon on the Mount), Matt. 5-7.

2. Jesus is the key to all facets of the sacrificial system in the old covenant.

    a. He is the *Passover sacrifice*, 1 Cor. 5.7.

    b. He is the *High Priest* depicted in the Old Testament Day of Atonement, Heb. 9.13-14; 10.11-14.

    c. He *transcends the Aaronic priesthood*, being after the high priestly order of Melchizedek, Heb. 7.1-28.

    d. He is the *fulfillment of the Temple* (he associates his body with the Temple itself), John 2.18-22.

3. Jesus is associated with the very person and work of God in the Old Testament.

    a. He is Lord upon his throne, the vision of Jehovah given to Isaiah.

        (1) Isa. 6.1-13

        (2) Cf. John 12.37-41

    b. As the Word made flesh, Jesus represents the final and authoritative revelation of God to humankind and to the universe.

        (1) John 1.18

        (2) Heb. 1.1-3

        (3) John 14.6

2

II. The Word Convinces Us of the Truth through its Outline of God's Kingdom Plan in Covenant with Abraham and Fulfillment in Jesus Christ.

A. Jesus is the subject that ties together both testaments of Scripture.

1. According to John the Apostle, Jesus Christ came into the world that he might destroy the works of the evil one, 1 John 3.8.

2. Because of Adam and Eve's rebellion in the Fall, humankind has been made a slave to sin, set under a curse, and made subject to the fear and tyranny of death (both physical death as well as separation from God).

3. But, because of God's lovingkindness and mercy, he sent his Son to pay the penalty of our sin, and destroy the Devil's claim on humankind and creation, Titus 2.11-14.

B. God's plan to redeem humankind was revealed in covenant with Abraham.

1. God made a covenant promise to Abraham, Gen. 12.1-3.

   a. To make of him a great nation

   b. To bless him and make his name great

   c. To bless those who blessed him and to curse those who cursed him

   d. In Abraham all the families of the earth would be blessed.

2. God's intent to restore all humankind in Abraham's seed has been fulfilled in Jesus Christ, Gal. 3.13-14.

3. Now through Abraham's seed and God's anointed one, Jesus Christ, God's cosmic plan is being fulfilled. In Jesus, God is restoring his kingdom rule throughout the universe, Col. 1.13-14.

C. For this outline of God's salvific work, no more authoritative, reliable, or sufficient witness exists than the sure Word of God.

1. God absolutely never alters his Word or covenant promise, Ps. 89.34-35.

2. God, in contradistinction to human beings, never lies nor fails to carry through on his promise, Num. 23.19.

3. God's immutability (that is, unchanging nature) ensures that the Word of God is an absolutely credible source for understanding his mind and will.

   a. Mal. 3.6

   b. Matt. 24.35

   c. James 1.17

III. God's Word Convinces Us of the Truth through the Witness of the Prophets and Apostles, God's Inspired Messengers of the Truth. God's Revelation of the Word Has Been Communicated through the Prophets, through Jesus Christ, and through His Appointed Messengers, His Apostles.

A. God spoke in times past through *the prophets*.

1. God spoke through the prophets to his chosen people, Heb. 1.1.

2. God's speaking through the prophets contained the master outline of his intent to save humankind, 1 Pet. 1.10-12.

B. God has spoken to the world perfectly and finally *through Jesus Christ*.

1. Jesus is God's final revelation to humankind, Heb. 1.2.

2. Jesus alone is the sole revealer of the Father's glory, John 1.18.

3. No other source of revelation is as sufficient as Christ, Col. 2.8-10.

C. Jesus entrusted his authoritative message of hope to *the Apostles*.

1. Directly chosen to be with Christ and to preach in his name, Mark 3.13-15

2. John 17 provides great insight into the unique role of the Apostles as communicators of God's revelation. As his chosen messengers, Jesus invests the Apostles with unique authority and witness, and states that:

 a. He revealed the Father's name to them.

 b. All that the Father had given to Jesus was made known to them.

 c. Jesus had given the Apostles the Father's saving word of truth.

 d. The Apostles' words concerning Christ would be the means through which the world would come to believe.

3. The Church has given the name "apostolicity" to this principle of the importance of the Apostles in the life and faith of the Church.

4. The Apostles' word, as representative of Jesus himself, holds authoritative status in the Church's understanding of Jesus' person and work.

 a. Paul suggests that the household of God is "built on the foundation of the Apostles and prophets, Christ Jesus himself being the cornerstone," Eph. 2.20.

 b. Defend the apostolic deposit: "contend for the faith that was once for all delivered to the saints," Jude 1.3.

 c. Terrifying consequences exist for those teaching things contrary to the Apostles' doctrine, Gal. 1.8-9.

2

d. Paul passes on to the Corinthians the apostolic deposit of the Gospel, i.e., what he received from Christ and his Apostles, which gives it final authority and full reliability, 1 Cor. 15.1-8.

5. The New Testament Scriptures are the word of the Apostles in written form, and therefore they carry the authority of Christ for those who believe, 2 Pet. 3.15-16.

Conclusion

» The Word of God convicts us of the truth.

» The Word of God's ability to convict regarding the nature of truth, and therefore learn of its capacity to transform our lives and perspectives through the Holy Spirit.

» Jesus of Nazareth is the central theme of God's revelation, and his message of the kingdom story serves as the backdrop of teaching throughout Scripture.

» God's Word possesses supreme integrity through its association with Jesus, and with the inspired prophets and Apostles.

The following questions were designed to help you review the material in the second video segment. They are designed to help you review the critical concepts associated with the Word of God's ability to convict regarding the truth of Jesus Christ, the Kingdom of God, and the integrity of the prophetic and apostolic witness to the faith. Please be clear and concise in your answers, and where possible, support with Scripture!

1. How does Jesus' high priestly prayer in John 17 help us understand the nature of the Word of God in relation to helping us comprehend the truth?

2. What biblical evidence do we have to suggest that Jesus Christ himself is the master theme of the Bible?

Segue 2

Student Questions and Response

3. In what specific ways do we know that Jesus is, in a very real sense, the fulfillment of the Old Testament sacrificial system of approach to God?

4. How is the person of Jesus intimately associated with the revelation of the Father throughout the Old Testament? What is his unique role in revealing (making known) to us the Father?"

5. How does the story of God's covenant faithfulness to Abraham help us understand the truth of Scripture concerning God's work in the world?

6. How does God's revelation through the three-fold messenger group (i.e., the prophets, Jesus Christ, and the Apostles) help convince us that the Scriptures are true, that is, they are reliable and valid witnesses of what God has done and will do in the world?

Summary of Key Concepts

This lesson has focused on the Word of God's ability to produce conviction at various levels, all of which lead us into a deeper, richer, and more nuanced relationship with God through Jesus Christ. The Word of God convicts us of sin, righteousness, judgment, and the truth.

☛ The Word of God is the instrument of the Holy Spirit that he uses to convict the world of sin, righteousness, and judgment.

☛ The Scriptures teach that sin includes anything that is out of sync with God's perfect character, law, and will. Sin and its effects touch all humankind, being both universal in scope and corrupting in its character.

☛ The moral Law of God, as a significant part of God's Word, convicts us of our sin, revealing the distance between our actions and the moral responsibility of God's holy demands.

☛ The Word of God convicts regarding righteousness. It reveals our inadequacy in keeping God's Law, and as well as God's righteousness by faith through the death and resurrection of Jesus Christ.

☛ The Word of God convicts regarding judgment, detailing accurately and powerfully God's intent to judge all humankind, whether living or dead, according to their deeds. In the consummation of the age, God will also judge Israel and the nations, the Church, Satan and his angels, and all the wicked dead.

↦ Being intimately connected to God's person through Jesus Christ, the Word of God produces conviction regarding the nature of truth, i.e., what is true concerning God, his work in the world, and the destiny and purpose of humankind.

↦ Jesus Christ himself is the master theme and the primary subject of the Scriptures, the fulfillment of the Old Testament sacrificial system, and the sole revealer of the invisible God's triune glory.

↦ God's kingdom plan is revealed in Scripture through God's faithful covenant promise to Abraham, and its fulfillment in the person of Jesus Christ. God's Word convicts us of the truth of his intent to save from among all the families of the earth a people for himself through Jesus Christ.

↦ The integrity of God's Word is underpinned through the integrity of God's chosen messengers, the prophets and the Apostles, who were given the task to represent and to speak of God's person and plan.

Student Application and Implications

Now is the time for you to discuss with your fellow students your questions about the Word of God and its ability to convict of sin, righteousness, judgment, and the truth. Ministering in urban America demands the possession of this Word, which penetrates and works deeply in the heart of those who hear it to convince of its integrity and truth. In thinking upon the convicting power of the Word, what particular questions do you have in light of the material you have just studied? Maybe some of the questions below might help you form your own, more specific and critical questions.

* Must the teacher or preacher believe the Word of God in order for it to convict others of sin, righteousness, judgment, and the truth? Explain your answer.

* Does the Word of God produce the same level of conviction in the believer as the unbeliever? How so? Cite examples.

* Does the Holy Spirit ever produce conviction of sin, righteousness, and judgment apart from the Word of God? Why or why not?

*   Does presentation style or the manner in which the Word of God is preached or taught affect its convicting power? How so?

*   What practical ways can we help others to understand that Jesus Christ himself is the master theme and primary subject of the Scriptures? Can something be convincing spiritually speaking and it not relate in some way to Jesus Christ? Explain your answer.

*   Why is it necessary to believe in the integrity of the Apostles and the prophets in order to hold that the Scriptures are true and reliable witnesses to God's work in Christ?

*   Why is it absolutely critical to understand Scripture's ability to convict others as one ministers to the lost in the city?

CASE STUDIES

Is Christianity Unique among All the Religions?

1   In honor of multi-cultural development and cooperation among religions in the community, you have been invited to come and share your view about "the nature of religious truth in a pluralistic society." In other words, in a community where so many different kinds of religion are practiced and believed, what does it mean to "seek and tell the truth" as a Christian believer? Some of your colleagues believe you should go and simply say that all other religions are false; only Christianity is true, Christ is Lord, and that's it. You want to be as clear about your faith as possible, while, at the same time, remaining sensitive to the purpose of the program, which isn't preaching but sharing your view. How would you go about sharing the beliefs of the Scriptures in this setting, especially about Christianity's claim of Jesus' unique place among all those claiming to speak for God.

Whatever Became of Sin?

2   One of the young adults in the church asks to speak to you about the subject of "sin." As a social worker for the state, she has repeatedly been told not to allow her own personal religious faith to interfere with her job of offering counseling and information to her "clients," many of whom are from the projects and who desperately need to know Christ. One of the main reasons for these restrictions came out recently in a discussion where her supervisor called into question the idea of "sin" altogether. In defending his position against sin, the supervisor said that "sin" is merely the idea of certain religious groups putting their narrow morality on the rest of us. No one can claim that something is sinful, since "sin" only means something within a context of a religious group. What would you counsel this young social worker regarding the idea of "sin" here?

Whose Righteousness Is Most Righteous?

After a long and heated conversation with a Jehovah's Witness, one of your church members found himself stumped at one of the arguments given against the Church. In comparing the level of quality of life of the Jehovah's Witness to average church goers, the Witness suggested that "Although there is much talk about righteousness in the Church, for the most part, you can do whatever you want and still be okay. As a matter of fact, I used to attend a church where the musicians fooled around sexually, one of the deacons exploded and cussed out the pastor in a business meeting, and the youth minister was separated from his wife. Nobody said anything about these situations, either. Since I have been a Jehovah's Witness, though, we actually live righteous among each other, and won't tolerate anyone living unrighteously." Your church member knew of situations like this, and was really thrown back by the argument. How would you advise him to answer arguments like this in the future, when he encounters such claims about righteousness?

Keeping the Main Thing the Main Thing

Recently, you have just been appointed Superintendent of the Sunday School for the church, and you are in the process of selecting teachers for the various age level classes you offer. You have looked back over the last year and one half of teaching and found there to be no one subject that the classes focus or concentrate on. All kinds of issues and subjects are being discussed at the various age levels, and none of them seem too interested in focusing on abstract, theological subjects. Most of the teachers select topics like, "Managing Your Money," or "Living Pure before God," or "Getting a Better Prayer Life." You are concerned that very little teaching about Jesus Christ and his work is being done, and you want to have a meeting with the teachers to cover how to do that. How might you approach this issue with your teachers, without creating in them a sense of guilt over the other topics and approaches they are accustomed to?

Restatement of the Lesson's Thesis

The Word of God convicts of sin, righteousness, judgment, and the truth. In regards to sin, the Word teaches that sin is both universal in its scope and corrupting of humankind in its character. In regards to righteousness, the Word of God testifies of God's perfect righteousness, and his gracious gift of righteousness to believers through the death and righteousness of Jesus Christ. In regards to judgment, God will judge all people according to their deeds. His final judgment will be comprehensive, including Israel and the nations, the Church, Satan and his angels, along with those who died who did not believe in Jesus Christ. Finally, the Word of God convicts us in regards to truth. Jesus Christ is the primary subject of the Scriptures, with God's kingdom plan through Abraham serving as the backdrop of God's work. The Word's truthfulness is grounded upon the ministry of the prophets, Apostles, and Jesus Christ, making our Bible absolutely reliable for all matters of faith and practice.

Resources and Bibliographies

If you are interested in pursuing some of the ideas of *The Word that Convicts*, you might want to give these books a try:

Pinnock, Clark H. *Biblical Revelation: Foundation of Christian Theology.* Chicago: Moody Press, 1971.

Smart, J. D. *The Interpretation of Scripture.* London: SCM press, 1961.

Young, E. J. *Thy Word is Truth.* London: Banner of Truth, 1963.

Ministry Connections

This is where you get an opportunity to explore specific, direct application of the insights of the lesson to your own very real practical ministry situation. The convicting power of the Word of God has application for all of our lives, and perhaps especially has bearing on some aspect of your work in your church, or in your ministry on behalf of your church. To begin with, what about your own life-is the Word of God convicting you of the truth? Is there an area in your life that the truth of God needs a greater and clearer place? Are you understanding the Word of God more and more, and is it producing in you the kinds of attitudes and perspectives it ought? What about those to whom you minister-are they experiencing more and more a greater understanding of the Word of God? Do you need to seek the Lord's grace for them-do they need a word of conviction in some area of their lives? What in particular is the Holy Spirit suggesting to you in regards to "the Word that convicts," for you, your family, your church, your ministry? What particular situation comes to mind when you think about how you might trust God for a greater sense of the convicting power of the Scriptures in your life?

2

This lesson has emphasized the direct relationship between the Word of God and the Spirit of God. In order for the Word of God to have its full sway in our lives, we must ask God to teach us his Word by his Spirit, to convict our own hearts of any sin, pride, foolishness, and resistance that might be in us, and then, that he would allow that same powerful Word to touch the lives of those for whom we pray and minister. Never underestimate the power of the Word of God to melt a waxy heart or turn a person from their own self-destructive path to the Lord. Pray that God would give you greater conviction about its inspiration, inerrancy, and potent power. Only as we experience the convicting power of the Word of God will we understand its ability to heal, to transform, and to illumine the hearts of others.

Counseling and Prayer

ASSIGNMENTS

John 16.7-11

Scripture Memory

To prepare for class, please visit *www.tumi.org/books* to find next week's reading assignment, or ask your mentor.

Reading Assignment

Again, make certain that you read the assignments above, and as last week, write a brief summary for them and bring these summaries to class next week (please see the "Reading Completion Sheet" at the end of this lesson). Also, now is the time to begin to think about the character of your ministry project, as well as decide what passage of Scripture you will select for your exegetical project. Do not delay in determining either your ministry or exegetical project. The sooner you select, the more time you will have to prepare!

Other Assignments

Our next study, lesson three of our Conversion and Calling module, is entitled, "The Word that Converts." In our next session we'll discover how the Gospel of Jesus Christ is the Word that converts, which leads both to *metanoia*, (repentance from sin and a turning towards God in Jesus Christ) and to *pistis*, (to faith through which God saves, delivers, and rescues the believer from the penalty, power, and presence of sin). This Word that converts produces inward signs of new spiritual life

Looking Forward to the Next Lesson

2

CONVERSION AND CALLING Capstone Curriculum / 6 7

within the believer, including a knowledge of God as heavenly Father, a new experience of prayer, an openness to the Word of God, and a willingness to follow the inner leading of Jesus' voice. We'll see further how outward signs also appear including an identification with the people of God, the display of a new Christlike character and lifestyle, a love for other believers, and a desire to see the lost won to Christ.

2

CONVERSION AND CALLING Capstone Curriculum / 6 7

Name _____

Date _____

For each assigned reading, write a brief summary (one or two paragraphs) of the author's main point. (For additional readings, use the back of this sheet.)

Reading 1

Title and Author: _____ Pages _____

Reading 2

Title and Author: _____ Pages _____

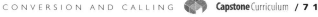

LESSON 3

The Word that Converts

Lesson Objectives

Welcome in the strong name of Jesus Christ! When you have completed your work in this module, we trust that you will be able to understand, articulate, and defend the truth that:

- The Word that converts is synonymous with the good news of salvation by faith in Jesus Christ. The Gospel of Jesus Christ is the Word that converts.

- This potent Word effectively leads us to *metanoia*, that is, repentance from sin and a turning towards God in Jesus Christ.

- This Word which works so effectively repentance (*metanoia*) to salvation, works with the same power to produce faith (*pistis*) in the believer. This faith saves, delivers, and rescues the believer from the penalty, power, and presence of sin.

- The Word of God, once activated by repentance and faith, produces confirming signs of God's forgiveness and the Holy Spirit's power in the life of the believer.

- Inwardly, the believer displays signs of new life in Jesus Christ including a knowledge of God as heavenly Father, a new experience of prayer, an openness to the Word of God, and a willingness to follow the inner leading of Jesus' voice.

- Outwardly, and in a corresponding way, the Word that converts produces outward signs including such things as an identification with the people of God, the display of a new Christlike character and lifestyle, a love for other believers, and a desire to see the lost won to Christ.

Devotion

You Simply Must Be Born Again

Read John 3.1-21. Of all the great marvels of Jesus' kingdom teaching we learn of and enjoy, perhaps none are as moving as his teaching about the need to be born from above, being born again. The experience of childbirth provides us with a window into the supernatural. For a tiny life to be born into the world, with friends and family joyfully welcoming this new life into the world, into their world, is a remarkable and joyous time. Jesus used the analogy of new birth to instruct us on the reality of new life through faith in him. The birth metaphor speaks of new genetics, an entirely new source of parental material and life potential. To be born again is to consider entirely new possibilities of life, new directions of growth, and new chances for transformation. To enter the Kingdom of God one must be born again, born from above, becoming sharers in the very DNA of God. When Jesus first declared this radical kingdom teaching, Nicodemus had no idea that he was speaking of the Holy Spirit and the Word of God. Flustered and confused, Nicodemus asked about how an old fellow might climb back into the womb of his mother in order to pass through the birth canal. He did not have a clue of the fundamental teaching Jesus was giving about spirituality. To receive eternal life, to enter into relationship with God, one must literally be born again spiritually by faith in Jesus Christ. Trusting in him, God uses the Word of God as spiritual seed which creates a brand new nature in the believer, a nature that comes directly from God through the Holy Spirit.

The Word of God produces conversion in the new believer's life; it does more than simply reform or adjust someone's life--it transforms it entirely. When Christ enters the heart of the converted one by faith, he/she is born again, with the potential to display all the characteristics of the One who brought forth that new life. This is why Christian commitment can never be summarized by external obedience to commands or outward conformity to tradition. God's intent is to create and display new life in the believer, his very own life becoming the ground and source of the Christian's service and faith. We share our parents looks, potential, and characteristics. If we are born from the Father, we, too, will look like him, reflect his image, and share his life.

Look at Jesus' good Word again:

> *John 3.3-6 - Jesus answered him, "Truly, truly, I say to you, unless one is born again he cannot see the Kingdom of God." [4] Nicodemus said to him, "How can a man be born when he is old? Can he enter a second time into his mother's womb and be born?" [5] Jesus answered, "Truly, truly, I say to you, unless one is born of water and the Spirit, he cannot enter the Kingdom of God. [6] That which is born of the flesh is flesh, and that which is born of the Spirit is spirit."*

Only faith in the Word of the Gospel concerning Jesus Christ can produce new life in the believer. How about you? Do you show the resemblance, those characteristics which prove you to have "your Father's eyes," that show you to have been born into the family of God by faith in Jesus Christ? "You must be born again!"

Nicene Creed and Prayer

After reciting and/or singing the Nicene Creed (located in the Appendix), pray the following prayers:

> *Eternal God and Father of our Lord Jesus Christ, we call you "Abba!" for you are our Papa by faith in your Son. Through faith in the Gospel of Jesus Christ, you have converted us, given us new life, transformed us by recreating your very own life within us. What can we say, now that you have made us your very own children? Our single desire is to become like you, Father, to be like our Elder Brother, the Lord Jesus, and obey you to the uttermost, to please you in all things, to reflect your image in everything we do. Fill us with your Spirit that we may give signs of being converted by you day by day, until we become more and more like your Son. Through Jesus Christ our Lord, Amen!*

> *Dear Lord God, I am Thy Creature—fashioned by Thee and placed here by Thy will. I have suffered grievous difficulties and borne great trials. Give me Thy grace that I may truly recognize that I am Thine and that Thou art my Father. May I wait upon Thee for help and security. Amen.*

~ Martin Luther. *Devotions and Prayers of Martin Luther.* Trans. Andrew Kosten. Grand Rapids: Baker Book House, 1965. p. 27.

3

Quiz

Put away your notes, gather up your thoughts and reflections, and take the quiz for Lesson 2, *The Word that Convicts.*

Scripture Memorization Review

Review with a partner, write out and/or recite the text for last class session's assigned memory verse: John 16.7-11.

Assignments Due

Turn in your summary of the reading assignment for last week, that is, your brief response and explanation of the main points that the authors were seeking to make in the assigned reading (Reading Completion Sheet).

 CONTACT

Too Religious for Me

 In becoming acquainted with one of his neighbors, Hosea learns that they used to be very involved in Christian activities and church going. For many years, this neighbor family attended a church which emphasized outward signs of inward faith.

In other words, they focused on doing good works to show that you truly belonged to God. As a disciplined and interested family, this neighbor household was very involved in all aspects of church life--choir and worship ministry, Christian education, and nursery duty, to name a few. Then, this church hired a new pastor who began to teach that busyness in the church was not sufficient for a relationship with God. One had to be converted, to be born again. This new emphasis was difficult for the neighbor family to accept, since they believed that they should practice religion by what they did. The born again language confused them. The neighbor father put it this way, "Being born again--that's becoming a little too religious for me!" What would you advise Hosea to say to his neighbor to clarify the relationship of faith to works in and through the church?

The Proof Is in the Pudding

In visiting a friend's church, Shirley was stunned to see the emphasis in the church on finances--on getting money and giving money. The current sermon series was on giving in order to get from God. One thing that the pastor said caused her to wonder if it were biblical teaching or not. The pastor said that if you were not willing to support your church and your pastor financially then you were probably not saved, and needed to check your faith credentials all over again. In powerfully strong terms and tones, the pastor boomed, "The proof is in the pudding. Just saying you are a Christian isn't enough; you have to prove precisely what you believe by how you act and what you give. I would say that if you meet a stingy so-called Christian, they probably aren't truly saved. To know God is to be generous, especially financially so!" How would you help Shirley evaluate the teaching she heard on that visiting Sunday?

Once Saved, Always Saved

James believes that sometimes the teaching of "eternal security" (the doctrine that once one is truly saved by faith in Jesus Christ, that they cannot ever be lost again) has been used as a smokescreen for practicing evil. As a Sunday School teacher, James is deeply concerned about "putting feet to our faith," not merely saying words but living out the reality of our faith in practical deeds and an active lifestyle. Convinced by texts like James 2.14-26 and Ephesians 2.10, James emphasizes that we can only know those who are legitimately converted by their good deeds and outward works. He has noticed that some who hold to the "once saved, always saved" position do not always show the kind of energy and commitment that he believes Christians ought to show. He happens to believe, however, that the heart of that teaching is correct. James holds that the one who repents and believes in Jesus is born again and receives eternal life. Still, why do so many who say they believe show little or no signs of it? He is somewhat confused and discouraged. How would you help James understand the relationship between professing faith and demonstration of your faith in life?

CONTENT ▶ **The Word that Converts**

Segment 1

Rev. Dr. Don L. Davis

Summary of Segment 1

This segment inquires into the relationship between God's Word and the power to be converted and transformed. In this study we will learn how the Gospel of Jesus Christ is the Word that converts. This transforming Gospel of Jesus Christ effectively leads us to *metanoia*, that is, to a true repentance from sin and a turning towards God in Jesus Christ. Furthermore, we will see how this same Gospel that produces repentance in the believer also moves us toward faith. The Word that leads us to repentance also leads us to faith (*pistis*), a living faith through which God saves, delivers, and rescues the believer from the penalty, power, and presence of sin.

Our objective for this first segment of *The Word that Converts* is to enable you to see that:

- The Word of God, the Word that converts, corresponds directly with the good news of salvation by faith in Jesus Christ. The Gospel of Jesus Christ is the Word that converts, making plain the conditions of salvation in Christ.

- The Word that converts produces repentance (*metanoia*), a turning from sin and idolatry to faith in Jesus Christ. This repentance includes (among other things) a change of mind, a godly sorrow for sin, and a confessing and forsaking of one's sins before the Lord.

- The Word that converts, that Word that produces repentance, is accompanied by saving faith in Jesus Christ as Lord, a deliberate dependence on Jesus Christ to save and redeem one's soul from the penalty, power, and presence of sin.

I. The Gospel of Jesus Christ Is the Word that Converts.

Video Segment 1
Outline

A. The Gospel of Jesus Christ, which is the power of God to salvation for both Jew and Greek, is a word regarding Jesus' sacrifice on the Cross.

    1. *Before the Cross*, the word of salvation came in the form of *expectation*, the hope of the Messiah's work, symbolized by the blood of animals sacrificed.

        a. The notion of "atonement" in the Old Testament deals with the concept of passing over, of sins "atoned for." The sacrificial system looked forward to the day when God's true Lamb would settle all accounts concerning sin and righteousness with God.

        b. Atonement can be understood through two critical passages in the New Testament.

            (1) Rom. 3.25 - "in his divine forbearance he had passed over former sins."

            (2) Acts 17.30 - "The times of ignorance God overlooked, but now he commands all people everywhere to repent."

        c. In this era, Jesus of Nazareth has now become our Passover, the One whose blood sacrifice on the cross atoned for our sins. Literally, in his death our sins are "passed over," 1 Cor. 5.7-8.

    2. *After the Cross*, the Word that converts is the Gospel of Jesus Christ.

        a. Jesus is the Lamb of God that takes away the sin of the world (i.e., through his sacrifice on the Cross), John 1.29.

b. Jesus canceled the record of our debt with its legal claims on the cross, Col. 2.14-15.

    c. The sacrifice of Jesus upon the cross is absolutely sufficient as a sacrifice for sin, Heb. 10.11-13.

3. Jesus died in the place of sinful humankind, bearing in his body our culpability and guilt, 1 Pet. 2.24.

4. The Word testifies to the universality of God's finished work in Jesus Christ.

    a. His was a work for the entire world.

       (1) John 3.16

       (2) Heb. 2.9

    b. His also was a work of mediation and redemption for the entire human race, 1Tim. 2.5-6.

    c. His was a work of *reconciliation* and *propitiation* for all humankind.

       (1) 2 Cor. 5.18-21

       (2) 1 John 2.2

B. Conversion is about the Word, not works.

1. Jesus suffered as God's Son once for our sins to bring us to God, 1 Pet. 3.18.

3

    a.   It is our faith in Christ that converts, not our appeal to our works of righteousness or obedience to God's Law.

    b.   Those who are righteous before God will live by faith, Rom. 1.16-17.

    c.   As believers, we walk by faith, not by sight, 2 Cor. 5.7.

2.   When we believe, we are delivered from our sin and justified before God by grace through faith (*sola gratia* - grace alone; *sola fides* - faith alone).

    a.   Eph. 2.8-9

    b.   2 Tim.1.8-10

    c.   Titus 2.11-14

C. God's work of conversion through the Word is experienced in three tenses of God's salvific work.

1.   We *have been delivered* (past tense) from the penalty of sin by Jesus' death on the Cross.

    a.   1 Cor. 1.18

    b.   Col. 1.13

2. We *are being delivered* (present tense) from sin's power through the Holy Spirit.

    a. Phil. 2.12-13

    b. Rom. 8.1-4

3. Ultimately, we *will be delivered* (future tense) from the very presence of sin at the Second Coming of Jesus Christ.

    a. John 14.1-4

    b. 1 John 3.1-3

II. The Word that Converts Effectively Leads Us to *Metanoia*, that is, to Repentance.

Biblical components of repentance:

A. Repentance involves *a change of mind*.

1. Matthew 21.28-29 shows this sense of repentance, of how the son changed his mind.

2. The prodigal son repented, he changed his mind and determined to return home to his father, Luke 15.17-18.

3. Peter charged the Jews at Pentecost to repent, to change their minds, and come to Jesus Christ, Acts 2.38.

B.　Repentance involves demonstrating *a godly sorrow for sin*.

　　1.　David expresses this sorrow in Psalm 38.18.

　　2.　In Jesus' parable of the Pharisee and the publican in Luke 18.9-14 the tax gatherer reveals the posture of godly sorrow, and the result of it.

C.　Repentance results in *confessing and forsaking sin*.

　　1.　The prodigal son, Luke 15.18

　　2.　The tax gatherer, Luke 18.13

　　3.　Confessing *and* forsaking of sin, Prov. 28.13

　　4.　*Turning from one's wicked ways*, Isa. 55.7

D.　Repentance involves a *turning to God in Christ from idolatry and futility*.

　　1.　Turning from darkness to light, from the power of Satan to God, Acts 26.18

　　2.　Turning *to God* from *idols*, 1 Thess. 1.9

E.　Repentance as a movement leads to a desire for *restitution* and *restoration*.

1. *Zaccheus* reveals true repentance when he affirms his desire to make up for his wrong in restitution, Luke 19.8-9.

2. The *prodigal son*, in response to his repentance, is restored to full relationship with the father, Luke 15.21-24.

III. The Word that Converts, the Word that Leads Us to Repentance, also Leads Us to Faith (*Pistis*), Heb. 11.1.

A. Hear the apostolic witness concerning God's work in Jesus of Nazareth, 1 Cor. 15.1-5.

1. Jesus was born of a virgin (incarnated).

2. Jesus lived in the world according to God's will.

3. Jesus suffered in his passion.

4. Jesus died on the cross.

5. On the third day, Jesus was raised from the dead.

6. After he arose, he was seen among many witnesses.

B. Confess that Jesus Christ is Lord, Rom. 10.9.

3

1. Jesus Christ has died and has been exalted to God's right hand, Phil. 2.9-11.

2. Jesus has been given a name above every name, both in this age and the age to come, and he made him head of the Church, Eph. 1.19-23.

C. Affirm the faith that God Almighty raised Jesus Christ from the dead, Rom. 10.9.

D. On the basis of this confession and belief, God imparts to us eternal life by grace alone (*sola gratia*) through faith alone (*sola fides*).

   1. John 16.7-11

   2. John 1.12-13

   3. 1 John 5.11-13

Conclusion

» The Word that converts is synonymous with the good news of salvation by faith in Jesus Christ. The Gospel of Christ is the Word that converts.

» This dynamic Word effectively leads us to *metanoia*, that is, to repent from sin and empty religious works to faith towards God in Jesus Christ.

» This Word produces in us faith (*pistis*), the medium through which God saves, delivers, and rescues the believer from the penalty, power, and presence of sin.

Segue 1

Student Questions and Response

Please take as much time as you have available to answer these and other questions that the video brought out. The Word that converts is the Gospel of Jesus, which leads us to repentance and faith, to salvation in Jesus Christ. To know and understand these concepts is critical for ministry and discipleship, especially the reformation ideas of *sola gratia* (by grace alone) and *sola fides* (by faith alone). Be clear and concise in your answers, and where possible, support with Scripture!

1. Why is it necessary for an unbeliever to experience new life within, and not merely an outward change of lifestyle in order to begin a relationship with God in Christ?

2. What is the relationship between the Word of God in the Gospel and the conversion of the new believer? Why is it necessary to believe the good news concerning Christ in order to be saved by God?

3. What is the biblical meaning of the term *metanoia*? What are some of the main biblical components to the idea of biblical repentance? Is it possible to have saving faith that does not include the act of repentance within it? Explain your answer.

4. What is the meaning of the term *sola gratia*? How does this term help us understand the nature of the Word that converts?

5. What is the definition given for *sola fides*? How does the Reformation doctrine ("by grace through faith alone") help us understand the way in which God converts the soul of the new believer by faith in Jesus Christ?

6. List out the specific items associated with the apostolic witness concerning Jesus Christ. How are we as believers to receive this witness that they give to the life, death, burial, and resurrection of Jesus Christ?

7. What are the three tenses associated with the redeeming and converting power of God in Jesus for the Christian? Can God save in one phase, and the believer be lost in another? Explain.

8. Why is it necessary to never conceive of repentance and faith as a work which the believer does to earn God's favor and forgiveness?

3

The Word that Converts

Segment 2

Rev. Dr. Don L. Davis

In this segment we hope to show how the Gospel of Jesus Christ, this converting Word of God, produces confirming signs of God's forgiveness and the Holy Spirit's power in the life of the believer. The Word that converts produces inward signs of life which serve as evidence to show the new convert's transformation in Jesus Christ. These include a knowledge of God as their heavenly Father, a new experience of prayer, an openness to the Word of God, and a willingness to follow the inner leading of Jesus' voice. In a corresponding manner, outward signs are also demonstrated by the believer in the Gospel of Jesus, including identifying with the people of God, displaying a new Christlike character and lifestyle and love for other believers, as well as showing a desire to see the lost won to Christ.

Summary of Segment 2

Our objective for this second segment of *The Word that Converts* is to enable you to understand, recite, and discuss the following truths:

- The Word that converts is a potent power, reproducing the very life of God in the heart and life of the Christian, shown inwardly and outwardly by signs (evidences) of the Sprit's working.

- This converting, life-birthing Word produces inward signs which provide inward assurance of the Spirit's working. These signs include a knowledge of God as one's Father, a new experience of prayer to God, an openness and hunger for the Word of God as nourishment, and a willingness to follow the inner leading of Jesus' voice as one's Shepherd.

- The Word of God also produces corresponding outward signs which the authentic Christian demonstrates, including a public association and identification with the people of God, the display of new desires, values and lifestyles through a new Christlike character, a love for other believers, and a growing desire to see the lost won to Jesus Christ.

3

Video Segment 2
Outline

I. The Word that Converts Produces Inward Signs of Life Which Serve as Evidence to Show Our Transformation in Jesus Christ.

2 Cor. 13.5

Examine yourselves, to see whether you are in the faith. Test yourselves. Or do you not realize this about yourselves, that Jesus Christ is in you? -- unless indeed you fail to meet the test!

A. One sign is a growing *inward assurance that God has become the heavenly Father* of the new believer.

   1. Eternal life is coming *to know the Father through his Son*, Jesus Christ, John 17.3.

   2. This must be *a work of God alone*, for no one can know God without the work of Jesus, Matt. 11.27.

   3. *The Spirit bears witness in the spirit of the believer* that they belong to the Father, Rom. 8.16-17.

   4. Those who belong to God will develop inside *an ever-increasing confidence that they belong to the Lord*, that the God and Father of Jesus Christ is their God, 1 John 3.19-24.

B. Another inward sign of authentic conversion is the *experience of conversing with God through prayer*.

   1. *The Holy Spirit comes to indwell the new believer by faith*, and his presence in the Christian produces a new desire to communicate with God. The Holy Spirit fills the Christian, enabling them to pray and worship God.

      a. Be *filled* with the Holy Spirit, Eph. 5.18-19.

3

b. *In everything give thanks* for this is God's will concerning you, 1 Thess. 5.16-18.

    2. The Holy Spirit *strengthens the inward prayer of the Christian* in deep spiritual ways, Rom. 8.26-27.

    3. We who are saved cry *"Abba, Father!"* (Aramaic, *"papa!"*) in our hearts, crying out to our Papa God to meet our needs, Rom. 8.15.

C. Another inward sign of conversion is the *openness to and hunger for the Word of God*.

    1. Like newborn babes, authentic believers desire *the pure milk of the Word of God*, the source of their strength and nutrition, 1 Pet. 2.2.

    2. *The teaching ministry of the Holy Spirit* produces new levels of discernment, hunger, and commitment to the Word of God.

        a. 1 Cor. 2.15

        b. 1 John 2.27

        c. John 16.12-15

    3. Through feeding upon the Word of God, the believer *increases in the knowledge of Christ*, 2 Tim. 1.12.

D. A final inward sign of conversion relates to the ability to *listen to Jesus Christ and follow him*. New believers recognize and follow the voice of the Savior.

    1. Those who know him will *listen to his voice and will not follow the voice of strangers*, John 10.1-6.

    2. Fellowship with God is based on *continuing to walk in the light*, and receiving cleansing through the blood for sin in one's life, 1 John 1.5-10.

    3. Those who belong to God *desire to follow God* and seek ways to respond rightly to his spoken and revealed will, 1 John 2.3-6.

II. The Word of God Produces in the Christian Outward Signs of Salvation Which Provide Evidence of Authentic Repentance and Faith.

3

A. A *strong association and identification with other Christians* - with the people of God as their new family and kinfolk.

    1. God's Word is a seed which produces "new birth" into the *family of God*.

        a. Unless we are born from above by the "water" and the Spirit, we cannot enter the Kingdom of God.

            (1) John 1.12-13

            (2) John 3.5

        b. The Word of God is the "*seed*" and "*engrafted word*" which produces in us the new birth, James 1.18, 21.

2. Cleansed by the life-giving Word, the new believer is *indwelt by the Holy Spirit and given a new nature* which is "renewed in knowledge after the image of its Creator."

   a. Col. 3.9-11

   b. Eph. 2.19

3. Having been born into God's family, new believers become *members of the household of God* and have a desire to grow and be with other believers, Gal. 3.26-28.

4. Those who have been authentically converted will not ignore the importance of fellowship, but will *identify and associate with the people of God as their own new people*, Heb. 10.24-25.

5. Those who *reject association with the body of Christ* prove themselves to be either worldly minded, or even not to belong to God at all, 1 John 2.19.

B. Those who have experienced the Word that converts will *display more and more the character of Jesus* in their lives.

   1. God's intent is to *conform all of his children to the image of his Son*.

      a. Rom. 8.28-29

      b. 2 Cor. 3.18

      c. Matt. 11.28-30

    2. The *fruit of the Spirit* becomes available to (i.e., is produced by the Holy Spirit within) the new believer by faith, Gal. 5.22-23.

    3. The *one possessing the hope of glory in Christ will purify him or herself* even as he did, 1 John 3.2-3.

C. The outward sign of *Christlike love and service to other believers.*

    1. By this shall all know you are My disciples, if you have *love*, John 13.34-35.

    2. The one who does not love, *does not know God*, 1 John 4.7-8.

    3. 1 John 3.14

D. The outward sign of *a publicly shown desire to share the Good News with the lost*, with those who do not know Christ.

    1. We will show *an ever-increasing readiness to share the Good News* with those who do not know him.

        a. Phil. 1.18

        b. *Be ready always* to give an answer of the hope that is in you, 1 Pet. 3.15.

3

2. We will *pour out our hearts in prayer for the lost*, Rom. 10.1.

3. We will be increasingly *willing to make great sacrifices* on behalf of those who are lost, that they might come to know the Lord, Rom. 9.1-3.

Conclusion

» The Word that Converts is a living dynamic Word that produces signs of new life, both inward and outward in the life of the truly believing Christian.

» This living Word produces abundant evidence within the heart of the Christian that they belong to God including the sure knowledge of God as one's Father, a new experience of prayer to God, an openness and hunger for the Word of God as nourishment, and a willingness to follow the inner leading of Jesus' voice as one's Shepherd.

» It also produces corresponding outward signs of the Word's converting power. Among other things, it produces a public association and identification with the people of God, the display of new desires, values and lifestyles through a new Christlike character, a love for other believers, and a growing desire to see the lost won to Jesus Christ.

The following questions were designed to help you review the material in the second video segment. The ability and power of the Word of God to produce in the believer genuine fruit is our hope and strength in ministry. We go forth in sharing God's Word because of the complete confidence we have in Scripture's ability to transform the life of the ones who embrace and believe it. Be clear and concise in your answers, and where possible, support with Scripture!

1. In what way does the Word of God change the relationship of the new believer with the Father? What kind of assurance will the new believer have about his/her new relationship with God through faith in Christ and the indwelling of the Spirit?

Segue 2

Student Questions and Response

2. How does Scripture describe the experience of prayer as a sign of being converted by the Word of God?

3. As a result of the Word of God's influence in a believer's heart, what kind of attitude and actions will occur in regards to their desire to understand God's Word and to follow Jesus' commands?

4. Must a person demonstrate any of these (or other) inward signs of conversion to claim that they belong to God? Is it possible to be converted and show no signs of change within? Why or why not?

5. What is the attitude of every true believer to the people of God, the Church? Is it possible to maintain an intimate relationship with God in Christ and be indifferent to other Christians? Why or why not?

6. What is the connection between loving Jesus and loving other believers? Explain.

7. The Word of God, when it produces conversions, changes the attitude of the believer regarding the lost. Explain how the Word of God changes the relationship of a new believer with those who do not know Jesus.

8. Can a person really claim intimacy with Jesus if they show no interest in seeing others come to know him? Explain your answer.

CONNECTION ▶

Summary of Key Concepts

This lesson focuses upon the Word of God's ability to create new life in the believer through repentance and faith, to deliver the believer from the effect and power of sin, and to produce within the heart and life new vital signs of the Spirit's presence and power. The Word converts, that is, it transforms the life of believers, drawing them to God, to Christ, and giving them a desire to glorify God through all aspects of their life.

☞ The Word that converts is synonymous with the good news of salvation by faith in Jesus Christ. The Gospel of Jesus Christ is the Word that converts.

☞ The Word of God leads the believer to *metanoia*, that is, repentance from sin and a turning towards God in Jesus Christ by faith in the Gospel.

3

- This Word which works so effectively repentance (*metanoia*) to salvation, also works the same power to produce faith (*pistis*) in the believer. Faith in God's Word is the means by which the Father saves, delivers, and rescues the believer from the penalty, power, and presence of sin.

- As a result of repentance and faith in the Word of God, new signs of God's forgiveness and the Holy Spirit's power are displayed within the heart and through the life of the believer.

- The inner life of the believer is transformed by the Word of God. Inwardly, the believer senses and experiences signs of new life in Jesus Christ including a knowledge of God as heavenly Father, a new experience of prayer, an openness to the Word of God, and a willingness to follow the inner leading of Jesus' voice.

- The Word of God is effective and active in also producing outward, concrete signs of new life in the Christian. These include (but are not necessarily limited to) such things as an identification with the people of God, the display of a new Christlike character and lifestyle, a love for other believers, and a desire to see the lost won to Christ.

- *Sola gratia* (by grace alone) and *sola fides* (through faith alone) are helpful Latin terms that summarize the nature of conversion through faith in the Gospel of Jesus Christ. We are saved by grace *through* faith alone, that is, through our reliance on the work of Jesus Christ on the cross. This grace and faith alone is the basis of redemption and forgiveness with God.

Student Application and Implications

Now is the time for you to discuss with your fellow students your questions about the nature of the converting power of the Word of God. Think carefully about your own ideas regarding the conversion through repentance and faith, and highlight these now in your discussion. What particular questions do you have in light of the material you have just studied? Maybe some of the questions below might help you form your own, more specific and critical questions.

* Can a person claim to know God intimately and show no inner or outward signs of being converted? Why is it critical for the one who claims to know God to demonstrate some sign of genuine conversion in their life?

* How precisely does the Word of God transform the attitude and actions of the person who believes? Is it necessary for us to know exactly how this process works in the heart? Why or why not?

* Why does it appear sometime as if the Word of God has no effect whatsoever in the life and attitude of people, even believers, at times? What is the problem if the Word is being taught and yet nothing seems to happen in anyone's life as a result?

* Should we expect some kind of change or reaction to occur every time we deliver God's Word to others, whether those who hear that Word are believers or not? Explain your answer.

CASE STUDIES

Is Repentance to be Understood as a "Work"?

1 As a Bible Study group at church studied the Gospel of Luke together, a fierce discussion arose among the members on the nature of repentance. Some began to argue that since we are saved by grace through faith alone, it is wrong to say that repentance is somehow separate from faith. They argued that whenever someone turns and trusts in Jesus, repentance is present in that trust. Others said that repentance was a separate action that came before faith. Others became more and more confused as the time went on, not really understanding the question, or even the importance of the argument. If you were assigned to help them understand the issues here, what would you teach them and what precisely would you do?

No Sign, No Salvation

2 God appears to be working tremendously through the new youth minister who has come to your church. More and more kids are coming to the ministry events, and many of the young people are making confessions of faith at the various worship concerts and evangelistic meetings hosted by the church. As the numbers have swelled, some have begun to wonder if many of the kids are there for other purposes than the Lord. Many of the kids continue to dress the same, many continue to smoke, and even cuss, while others appear to have changed entirely. How would you address the issues of change and conversion with the youth minister, if he/she asked you what you thought about what was going on?

How Long Will It Take?

Recently, three young men prayed to receive Christ in the park where a group of local skinheads meet. This particular group is deeply committed to racist views about so-called inferior races, but are especially vicious in their views about Blacks and Hispanics. Over the last three weeks, one can notice real changes in the lives of the guys as they have been coming to church and small group, but every now and then, you pick up that there still seems to be some residue of prejudice and racist attitudes in their behavior. Some in the body are skeptical about their conversion, while others defend them, that God is working in their lives and will continue to work as they grow in Christ. What kind of change can we expect in the lives of these young men, and, if it takes time to overcome, about how long will it take for them to overcome the bondage of the past in terms of racial prejudice?

"I Don't Feel Comfortable Doing That."

In a small group study for new members, a dear sister struggles every week in praying in public. She is shy, and likes to pray alone, but has a real problem praying out loud, in front of others. She is not convinced that prayer out loud is even necessary. "Didn't Jesus tell us to go to the closet and pray in private? Why is it so important to pray with others out loud, then?" What particular counsel would you give to this sister to help her understand that praying is one of the signs of conversion we should expect from all truly saved people? Is it even necessary for her to learn how to do this publicly? If she continues to refuse to pray, does that suggest she might not be saved? Why or why not?

The Gospel of Jesus Christ is the Word that converts. The Spirit of God uses the Word to produce *metanoia*, that is, repentance from sin and a turning towards God in Jesus Christ. This work also produces faith (*pistis*), which saves, delivers, and rescues the believer from the penalty, power, and presence of sin. The Word of God, once activated by repentance and faith, produces confirming signs of God's forgiveness and the Holy Spirit's power in the life of the believer. Inwardly, the signs include the knowledge of God as heavenly Father, a new experience of prayer, an openness to the Word of God, and a willingness to follow the inner leading of Jesus' voice. Outwardly, the Word creates an identification with the people of God, the display of a new Christlike character and lifestyle, a love for other believers, and a desire to see the lost won to Christ.

Restatement of
the Lesson's Thesis

3

Resources and Bibliographies

If you are interested in pursuing some of the ideas discussed in this lesson regarding the power of the Word of God to transform and convert, you might want to give these books a try:

Henrichsen, Walt. *Layman's Guide to Applying the Bible*. Grand Rapids: Zondervan Books, 1985.

Kuhatschek, Jack. *Applying the Bible*. Grand Rapids: Zondervan Books, 1990.

Lewis. C. S. *Mere Christianity*. New York: Macmillan Company, 1960.

Stott, J. R. W. *Understanding the Bible*. Glendale: Regal Books, 1972.

Ministry Connections

Seeking to relate these truths to your own ministry through your church represents the core of this teaching. In thinking about the converting power of the Word of God, what specific challenges, issues, or situations are you facing now in ministry where these truths must be applied and understood? In all the issues surrounding urban ministry, perhaps none are as important as this critical issue: our confidence and ability in handling the Word of God, and its ability to transform and convert the lives of those to whom we share it. Concentrate on the various ministry opportunities you are involved in, and ask the Holy Spirit to teach you where and how you might be able to rethink situations or issues in light of the teaching of this lesson on the Word of God. As you consider your ministry project for this module, you can possibly use it to connect to these truths in a practical way. Seek the face of God for insight, and come back next week ready to share your insights with the other learners in your class.

Counseling and Prayer

Undoubtedly you know of very specific examples and situations right now where you or those to whom you minister need to experience the converting and transforming power of the Word of God. It could be that some of these needs and situations have been made clearer through your study of the Word of God, and its ability to convert and transform. Do not hesitate to find a partner in prayer who can share the burden and lift up these specific requests for the Word's converting power in your life and the life of others. Always remember that your instructor is extremely open to walking with you on this. Be assured, also, that your church leaders (especially your pastor) may be specially equipped to help you answer any difficult questions arising from your reflection on this study. Be open to God and allow him to lead you as he determines. Ask God to confirm his Word in signs and

3

wonders right in your midst, and in the lives of those whom you minister. Claim God's specific promise of Isaiah 55.8-11, that God's Word cannot return void or empty in the purpose with which he sends it.

ASSIGNMENTS

Romans 10.8-13

Scripture Memory

To prepare for class, please visit *www.tumi.org/books* to find next week's reading assignment, or ask your mentor.

Reading Assignment

As usual you ought to come with your reading assignment sheet containing your summary of the reading material for the week. Also, you must have selected the text for your exegetical project, and turn in your proposal for your ministry project.

Other Assignments

In our final lesson we will look at the holy Word of God as *The Word that Calls*. We will learn how the Word calls us to discipleship, to live the adventure of his story in a committed life of discipleship. We are asked to make ourselves unconditionally available to Jesus that we might love him supremely, taking on the identity of aliens and sojourners in this world, as those who have become bondslaves to his glory. All that we are and have in this life should become devoted to knowing God and making him known as his bondslaves in this world. Furthermore, we'll explore how the Word of God calls us to live and work in community, to live free in Christ as an opportunity for love and evangelism, and to mission; fulfilling the Great Commission, doing battle with our spiritual enemy the devil, and demonstrating the life of the Kingdom through our love and good works.

Looking Forward to the Next Lesson

Name _____

Date _____

For each assigned reading, write a brief summary (one or two paragraphs) of the author's main point. (For additional readings, use the back of this sheet.)

Reading 1

Title and Author: _____ Pages _____

Reading 2

Title and Author: _____ Pages _____

The Word that Calls

Lesson Objectives

Welcome in the strong name of Jesus Christ! After your reading, study, discussion, and application of the materials in this lesson, you will be able to understand, articulate, and defend the truth that:

- The Word that effectively leads us to salvation and conversion also calls us to live as disciples of Jesus, obedient to his will.

- This Word that calls us to discipleship demands that we make ourselves available to Jesus that we might love him supremely, above all other loves, including marriage and family, in such a way that we may serve him as Lord above all.

- The call also asks us to embrace our new identity in Christ as aliens and sojourners in this world, those men and women who act and work as citizens of the Kingdom of God in the midst of the world, as representatives of Jesus.

- The lifestyle of discipleship is demonstrated when we respond favorably to the call to live as sacrificial servants to his glory. As slaves of Christ, we commit all we are and have to glorifying him and accomplishing his will in the world, as he directs.

- We are also called to live and work in community, as members of God's glorious family in the people of God (*laos*).

- The disciple of Jesus is called to live in the freedom of Jesus Christ, to use their freedom as an opportunity to fulfill the Great Commandment, and to give clear witness for the purpose of saving others for the cause of Christ.

- The word that calls to discipleship, community, and freedom also calls us to mission. As agents of the Kingdom of God, we are called to fulfill the Great Commission, to do battle with our spiritual enemy the devil, and to demonstrate the life of the Kingdom through our love and good works.

The Road We Travel

Read Matthew 4.17-22. What is your purpose in life, the ultimate concern, the supreme "why" behind all of the "whats," "whos," and "hows" in your life. No person can live a full rich life, or come to any kind of understanding of what they are to do without knowing what they have been called to, and what God demands of their specific, individual lives. Os Guiness, in his intriguing book *The Call*, speaks of this deep passion in the heart of everyone to come to find their ultimate purpose in life. "Deep in our hearts, we all want to find and fulfill a purpose bigger than ourselves. Only such a larger purpose can inspire us to heights we know we could never reach on our own. For each of us the real purpose is personal and passionate: to know what we are here to do and why. Kierkegaard wrote in his *Journal*: 'The thing is to understand myself, to see what God really wants me to do; the thing is to find a truth which is true *for me*, to find the *idea for which I can live and die*'" (Os Guinness, *The Call*. [Nashville: World Publishing, 1998, p.3]).

Jesus was preaching the reign of God come to earth, calling men and women to live for the Kingdom of God which had come in his person. Encountering Simon and Andrew, and James and John, two pairs of brothers who fished as a calling and vocation, our Lord called them to a higher, more true, and ultimate purpose. To follow Jesus as Lord, to respond to the Word of obedience that saves and disciples--this is the purpose of life. Jesus came to these men, shared simply his call for them to follow him, and his promise that he would make them fishers of men. He not only changed their job, he transformed their lives, and placed them on a road to travel that led to adventure, conversion, suffering, and witness. They simply heard his personal Word and responded in faith and obedience. That Word that called them to faith called them to discipleship, and through that Word, they discovered the meaning of life itself: to bring glory and praise to God alone through service to his Son, Jesus Christ.

Regardless of the road we travel today, if we listen we will hear the words of our Master continuing to go forth, even in the darkest alleys and streets of the city. Jesus is alive, and by his Holy Spirit he is calling men and women to himself to live as his servants, to grasp the adventure, to allow his Spirit to make their lives over again as they obey him day by day. The disciples of old (as all true disciples do) responded immediately to God with prompt obedience, genuine passion, and true longing. Even though they had families, responsibilities, duties, and jobs, they laid everything down in order to follow the One who alone could give them what nothing else can: eternal life.

4

In the midst of your travels, on your job, in your life, have you heard and responded to the call of God in Jesus Christ? Have you "immediately left all, and followed him" as the pair of brothers did? If you listen, you will hear him give you the same sovereign Word of command he gave to them. His promise is ever sure: "Follow me, and I will make you fishers of men." You no longer will live for yourself, but will live for his glory, and become a witness to others of his great and glorious salvation. Respond to his Word, become his disciple, give prompt obedience to his Word that calls you to himself, and that calls you to discipleship.

Nicene Creed and Prayer

After reciting and/or singing the Nicene Creed (located in the Appendix), pray the following prayers:

Eternal God, Father of our Lord Jesus Christ, we ask that your Son, the Living Lord, speak a word that would call us to you, that calls us to be your people and would sustain us with the power of your Spirit. We are called to discipleship, to community, to freedom, and to mission. Allow your holy and eternal Word to be heard in our midst, and give us the courage and passion to follow that Word with all our hearts, to serve you with joy, to persevere in the will of God, to please your heart and to bring you glory in the Church. Thank you for the Word that calls us to yourself. In Jesus Name, Amen.

We give thanks to Thee, Lord God Almighty, that Thou hast revived us through Thy heavenly gift. We pray that by Thy mercy we may attain to a firm faith in Thee and a fervent love for one another through Jesus Christ Thy Son our Lord. Amen.

~ Martin Luther. **Devotions and Prayers of Martin Luther**. Trans. Andrew Kosten. Grand Rapids: Baker Book House, 1965. p. 39.

4

Quiz

Put away your notes, gather up your thoughts and reflections, and take the quiz for Lesson 3, *The Word that Converts.*

Scripture Memorization Review

Review with a partner, write out and/or recite the text for last class session's assigned memory verse: Romans 10.8-13.

Assignments Due

Turn in your summary of the reading assignment for last week, that is, your brief response and explanation of the main points that the authors were seeking to make in the assigned reading (Reading Completion Sheet).

CONTACT

1

2

3

How Much Money Can a Christian Make?

In one of the men's discipling cell groups in a church, a heated debate has been brewing since they began a study in the Gospel of Luke. Luke 14.33 says "So then, none of you can be My disciple who does not give up all his own possessions." One brother interpreted this (along with other texts in the Bible) to say that it is impossible for a Christian to be wealthy, even to own things personally, for it says that he must give up all his possessions. Other brothers in the study suggest that this is simply too extreme an interpretation; the real idea is that they should be willing to give up all their possessions, not actually give them up. What is the real nature of discipleship that comes out in this conversation?

Date with Spouse versus Date with Service

The elders of the church meet every other Friday evening, which is the time that most of the men and women can attend. One dear brother determined that he would need to leave the elder board because Friday evenings for the last few years have been his date night with his wife. Since God would have him maintain the priority of marriage above the church, he argues, he simply can no longer serve on the Elders Council of church. The other members of the council argued that, in one sense, the Church and its affairs as God's community should take priority over the issues of marriage and family. The elder argued other Scripture, which suggest that the family must be held as a model of Christ and the Church. Whose side of the argument is most persuasive to you here?

Invite Them to Discipleship, Not to Salvation

A Baptist congregation just up the way is experiencing controversy over its worship services. The new pastor, a fine Christian and biblical teacher, believes that there can be no salvation where there has been no commitment to discipleship. The church, at the end of its services, invites those in the audience who have not responded to Christ to come to him in faith and obedience. Since the new pastor has arrived, he has preached strongly that if you refuse to acknowledge Jesus as your Lord then you cannot receive him as Savior. You receive Jesus as Savior and Lord, not one first and the other second. This seems to go against what some of the deacons have understood of "salvation by grace through faith," and borders on making salvation a work of the new Christian and not the gift of God. How ought we to understand the invitation to Christ-what does it mean?

4

The Word that Calls

Segment 1

Rev. Dr. Don L. Davis

Summary of Segment 1

This first segment explores the concept of the Word of God as a Word that calls to discipleship. God does not simply convert us to Christ, he calls us to live the adventure of his Story in a committed life of discipleship. The same Word that calls us to salvation through faith calls us to make ourselves unconditionally available to Jesus that we might love him supremely, above marriage and family, in such a way that we may serve him without conditions. We are to embrace our new identity in Christ, and this call to discipleship involves us taking on the identity of aliens and sojourners in this world, as those who seek to honor God and look for the new city of God in glory. The call to discipleship also includes God's command to us to become sacrificial servants to his glory. All that we are and have in this life become devoted to knowing God and making him known as his bondslaves in this world.

Our objective for this first segment of *The Word that Calls* is to enable you to see that:

- The Word that effectively leads us to salvation and conversion also calls us to live as disciples of Jesus, obedient to his will.

- This Word that calls us to discipleship demands that we make ourselves available to Jesus that we might love him supremely, above all other loves, including marriage and family, in such a way that we may serve him as Lord above all.

- The call also asks us to embrace our new identity in Christ as aliens and sojourners in this world, those men and women who act and work as citizens of the Kingdom of God in the midst of the world, as representatives of Jesus.

- The lifestyle of discipleship is demonstrated when we respond favorably to the call to live as sacrificial servants to his glory. As slaves of Christ, we commit all we are and have to glorifying him and accomplishing his will in the world, as he directs.

4

I. Like Jesus' Own Disciples, We are Called to Discipleship. The First Aspect of this Call Is God's Mandate to a Supreme Love for Jesus Christ.

Video Segment 1 Outline

A. This supreme love for Jesus Christ must transcend our love for marriage and family.

    1. Love for Christ must transcend love for siblings and parents, Matt. 10.34-37.

    2. Love for Christ must also transcend love for spouse and children.

        a. Matt. 10.37

        b. Luke 14.26

B. Our love for Christ must transcend our associations with the world and its pleasures.

    1. Do not lay up treasures for ourselves upon the earth.

        a. Matt. 6.19-21

        b. Luke 14.33

    2. This love will cause us to turn our backs on the fame and fortune associated with this life.

4

C. The call to discipleship involves persecution from those who hate the Lord.

    1. Matt. 10.22-25

    2. Acts 14.21-22

    3. 2 Tim. 3.12

    4. John 12.24-26

    5. 1 Pet. 2.21-25

II. The Call to Discipleship Means that We are Called to Live as Aliens and Sojourners in this World.

A. We are commissioned to shine as lights in this present evil world, Phil. 2.14-16.

    1. We are not of this present world system, John 17.14-18.

    2. We are called to be salt (the preservative that sustains and enriches life) and light (that force which illumines the way and exposes what is present).

        a. Matt. 5.14-16

4

     b. Eph. 5.8-14

     c. Rom. 13.11-12

3. We shine, we serve as lights in the world as we pass through it, not set up settlements of power here.

     a. 1 Pet. 2.11

     b. Heb. 11.16

B. The Word enlightens us on the futility of loving the world and the things in it, 1 John 2.15-17.

1. To love the world is to find oneself at cross-purposes with God, James 4.4.

2. We anchor our hope for a new heaven and earth where the righteousness of God will dwell, 2 Pet. 3.11-13.

3. As Jim Elliott, missionary to the Auca Indians of Ecuador said, "He is no fool who gives up what he cannot keep to gain what he cannot lose."

C. Living as an alien and stranger allows us to use the resources of the world for the glory of God without being overwhelmed by them.

1. As sojourners, we seek here no lasting place, so we are set free to go anywhere the Lord calls. We have no permanent address in this world.

2. As sojourners, we may relocate anywhere he wishes as we respond to his Spirit.

3. We long for our true home, which allows us maximum flexibility for communicating Jesus Christ to others.

III. The Call to Discipleship Also Involves a Call to Live as Sacrificial Servants to the Glory of Jesus Christ.

A. We have been called to bear fruit, and so the Father will be glorified.

1. The Father is glorified as we as Christ's disciples bear much fruit, John 15.8.

2. The fruit that we bear in Christ's name for the Father's glory is to be fruit that remains-lasting, enduring, and abundant fruit-in our lives, in our praise, and in our ministries, John 15.16.

B. In order to bring glory to God, we must embrace a lifestyle of sacrificial service, showing a willingness to die to ourselves in order that we might be free to live for Christ and his Kingdom alone.

1. We must be willing to sacrifice all else for his name's sake and glory, Phil. 3.7-8.

2. We are called to take up our cross daily and follow him.

4

    a. Luke 9.23

    b. Luke 14.27

    c. 2 Cor. 4.10-12

3. We have been crucified with Jesus Christ in order that now we might live as servants and bondslaves of God in this world.

    a. Gal. 2.20

    b. Gal. 6.14

    c. Rom. 6.3-4

C. Whether we live or die, we are the Lord's, and our desire must be to glorify him whether by life or by death.

1. None of us lives or dies for our own purpose, Rom. 14.7-9.

2. The mind of Christ (which was humble, self-forgetful and self-sacrificing) is to be reflected in us, Phil. 2.5-8.

3. Paul could say that whether by life or death, his only desire was that the Lord Jesus be glorified in his body, Phil. 1.20-21.

Conclusion

» The Word *calls us to discipleship*, to participate in God's grand kingdom story in a committed life of discipleship.

» We are called to *love Jesus supremely*, above marriage and family, in such a way that his glory and concerns take center stage in our lives.

» We are called to *live as aliens and sojourners in this world*, living free to be available to him however he leads us.

» We are called to *become sacrificial servants to his glory*, dying to ourselves that we might live to his glory.

Segue 1

Student Questions and Response

Please take as much time as you have available to answer these and other questions that the video brought out. Answer the questions below, make certain you grasp the critical ideas about how the Word calls us to live a radical life of discipleship, under the lordship of Jesus Christ. Be clear and concise in your answers, and where possible, support with Scripture!

1. What is the relationship between God's Word which calls us to repent and believe in Jesus Christ, and that same Word that calls to live as disciples of Jesus? Explain your answer.

2. What is involved in "loving Jesus supremely" above all other things, including marriage and family? How are we to understand one's allegiance to Jesus compared to other allegiances? Explain.

3. What is the connection between living faithful as a radical disciple of Jesus Christ and experiencing persecution? Is there any way we can avoid such persecution, and still be a disciple of Jesus?

4. What does it mean that we are to "embrace our new identity in Christ as aliens and sojourners in this world?" What does Scripture say about those who claim to be intimate with God and yet love the world and its evil systems?

5. As representatives of the coming Kingdom of God, to what extent should Christians seek to gain the world's riches, fame, and power? Explain carefully your answer.

4

6. What does it mean that God has called us to live as sacrificial servants to his glory?

7. What would be an example of what it means to "die to oneself" in order to live unto Christ? Does living as a bondslave of Jesus ensure that we will never become "rich and famous?" Explain your answer.

8. Explain the statement that "whether we live or we die, we are the Lord's." What is the attitude of the person who has died to themselves and have yielded themselves to God for his glory?

The Word that Calls

Segment 2

Rev. Dr. Don L. Davis

The Word that converted us and called us to discipleship, also calls us to live and work in community, as members of his glorious family in the people of God (*laos*). As members of the people of God, we are called to freedom, to use our liberty in Jesus Christ as an opportunity to fulfill the Great Commandment, that is, to love and serve others, as well as for the purpose of saving others for the cause of Christ. As members of God's family, as those called to discipleship, community, and freedom, we are also called to engage in the mission of the Kingdom. God the Father has called us to fulfill the Great Commission, to do battle with our spiritual enemy the devil, and to demonstrate the life of the Kingdom through our love and good works.

Our objective for this second segment of *The Word that Calls* is to enable you to see that:

- The same Word that calls us to live as disciples of Jesus individually also calls us to live and work in community, as members of his glorious family in the people of God (*laos*).

- As members of the family of God, we are called to live free in Jesus Christ, and to employ our liberty in Christ as an opportunity to love others, thus

Summary of Segment 2

4

fulfilling the Great Commandment, as well as seeking to save others for the cause of Christ.

- As free members of the people of God, we are called to mission. As 21st century disciples of Jesus, we are called to fulfill the Great Commission, to make disciples of all nations, to do battle with our spiritual enemy the devil, and to demonstrate the life of the Kingdom through our love and good works.

Video Segment 2 Outline

I. The Word of God that Calls Indeed Calls Us to Live and Work in Community, as Members of His Family, Living out the Story of God as His People (the *Laos* of God).

A. The Word of God that calls us to community causes us to share in the very life of God through *regeneration*.

1. *Palingenesia* - regeneration and "new birth." The power of the Word of God actually creates in us the very life of God, we become linked to God's own life-together.

a. We now have become partakers of the divine nature of God, sharing his very life, 2 Pet. 1.3-4.

b. We are members of God's people and family, 1 John 3.1.

c. That which is born of the flesh is flesh; that which is born of the Spirit (i.e., of God's own life) is spirit, John 3.5-6.

2. Believers have been joined together as one in the life of Jesus Christ.

4

a. We are now "in Christ" who becomes our source and our existence, Col. 3.4.

b. Regardless of our background, condition, or social history, through faith in Christ we have become one in Jesus Christ.

   (1) Gal. 3.28

   (2) Col. 3.11

3. Believers have experienced the washing of regeneration and renewal of the Holy Spirit (i.e., they now share God's spiritual DNA through Jesus Christ), Titus 3.5-6.

4. Through the Holy Spirit, we have become joined to the life of God in Christ, and share together in the one true life which fills up the people of God.

   a. 1 Cor. 12.13

   b. Eph. 1.13

   c. There is and has ever been only one body and one faith, and only one hope of our calling, Eph. 4.4-6.

   d. The Christian life is a communal life, a life that is born, raised, and matured in the context of Christian community.

B. Through regeneration, God implants us into his community through spiritual adoption.

1. We have been adopted into God's family by faith: *huiothesia* - "a placing" (combination of the Greek terms for "son" and for the verb "to place").

2. We have received the Holy Spirit, who is called "the Spirit of adoption" Rom. 8.15-16.

3. The Spirit of adoption has made us God's very own kin, his kids, and as his children, then heirs of God in Christ, Rom. 8.15-16.

C. This call to community through regeneration and adoption has several practical implications for us as Christians and Church leaders:

1. God calls us to live in community, not in isolation.

2. We have become members of the one true Church of all places and all times.

3. Authentic discipleship involves belonging to a local fellowship of believers.

4. Christian leadership is for the sake of edifying and empowering the Church to become all it has been called to become in Jesus Christ, Heb. 13.17.

5. The call to Christian maturity is a call to community, not merely a call to my own personal welfare to the exclusion of other disciples.

II. The Word Calls Us to Liberty in Christ as an Opportunity to Fulfill the Great Commandment, and for the Purpose of Saving Others for the Cause of Christ.

    A. Because of the all-sufficient work of Jesus Christ on the Cross, God calls all his disciples to live free, to liberty in Christ.

        1. It was for freedom that Jesus won the victory, and we ought not be entangled in any yoke of bondage.

            a. Christ has set us free through his death on the cross, Gal. 5.1.

            b. We were called to freedom, Gal. 5.13.

        2. Through the blood of Jesus, we have been liberated from all forms of self-righteousness and sinful bondage, John 8.31-36.

        3. Through faith in Christ we have received the Holy Spirit who has made us ministers of the new covenant, 2 Cor. 3.17.

    B. The dimensions and elements of the freedom we have in Christ.

        1. We have been set free from the guilt and condemnation of the Law, Rom. 8.1-4.

            a. In Jesus Christ we have been set free from all condemnation.

            b. Our flesh makes righteousness through the Law impossible.

4

    c.   The righteousness of the Law is being fulfilled in us, not by us, in the Holy Spirit.

2. We have been set free from empty efforts of dead works to please God on our own merit and strength.

    a.   We are saved by grace through faith, not of works, Eph. 2.8-9.

    b.   There remains a rest to children of God, that they now can cease from their dead works to serve God in truth, Heb. 4.9-10.

    c.   Our consciences have now been cleansed and purged because of the blood of Christ and God's acceptance of him on the cross, Heb. 9.13-14.

3. We have been set free from the devil's tyranny, especially his manipulation of the fear of death, Heb. 2.14-15.

    a.   Through the cross, Christ has made an open show of the principalities and powers, Col. 2.15.

    b.   The enemy can neither destroy or oppress us if we stand firm in the victory won by Christ for us.

        (1) James 4.7

        (2) 1 John 4.4

        (3) 1 Pet. 5.8-9

4

C. We are not to use our freedom as a license or cover for sin, but as an opportunity to fulfill the Great Commandment, i.e., love and care for others.

    1. Peter exhorts us not to use our freedom as a covering for evil, but rather to live as servants of God, 1 Pet. 2.16.

    2. Use your freedom as an opportunity to show love to all, but especially those of the household of faith, Gal. 5.13.

    3. God allows us to be free in order to love others.

        a. We are to become all things to all people in order to save them, 1 Cor. 9.19-23.

        b. We are free to use anything that is not outside the will of God to win others to him, 1 Cor. 3.21-23.

D. Purposes for which we are called to use our freedom in Christ.

    1. For the things that are *profitable*, 1 Cor. 6.12a - "All things are lawful for me, but not all things are helpful."

    2. Not for anything that is *injurious and addictive*, 1 Cor. 6.12b - "All things are lawful for me, but I will not be mastered by anything."

    3. Only for that which is *edifying*, 1 Cor. 10.23 - "All things are lawful, but not all things are helpful. All things are lawful, but not all things build up."

4. Not for anything that causes *a believer of weaker conscience to stumble*, 1 Cor. 8.13 - "Therefore, if food makes my brother stumble, I will never eat meat, lest I make my brother stumble."

5. Only for those things which provide *an opportunity to love our brothers and sisters in Christ*, Gal. 5.13 - "For you were called to freedom, brothers. Only do not use your freedom as an opportunity for the flesh, but through love serve one another."

6. For only those things which *glorify God*, 1 Cor. 10.31 - "So, whether you eat or drink, or whatever you do, do all to the glory of God."

7. Not for anything that gives *offense to Jew, Gentile, or the Church of God*, 1 Cor. 10.32 - "Give no offense to Jews or to Greeks or to the Church of God."

8. Only for those things which contribute to *winning others to Christ*, 1 Cor. 10.33 - "Just as I try to please everyone in everything I do, not seeking my own advantage, but that of many, that they may be saved."

III. The Word of God Calls Us - His People - to Engage in Mission, to Make Disciples of Jesus Christ among All Nations, to Engage in Spiritual Warfare against the Devil, and to Demonstrate the Life of the Kingdom through Our Love and Good Works.

A. As members of the universal priesthood, God calls us to fulfill the Great Commission.

1. The command to the Church is to go and make disciples of all nations, Matt. 28.18-20.

2. Begin at your own "Jerusalems" to our "Judeas" to our "Samarias," and go to the very "ends of the earth," Acts 1.8.

3. We are ambassadors of Jesus Christ, 2 Cor. 5.18-21.

    a. Everyone is to be ready to give anyone who asks a reason of the hope that is in us, 1 Pet. 3.15.

    b. All of us are to be equipped to share Christ in our circle of friends, family, and associates, ministering God's grace to others, 1 Pet. 4.10-11.

B. As members of God's army, God calls us to engage in spiritual warfare with our arch enemy, the devil.

    1. We are engaged in spiritual warfare against spiritual forces which seek to thwart God's Kingdom purpose in the world, Eph. 6.12-13.

    2. We are called to expose and refute the lies and deceptions of the enemy.

        a. The devil's intent is to thwart God's working in the world through the destruction and damage inflicted upon God's creation, especially human beings, John 10.10.

            (1) Blinds the minds of those who do not believe, 2 Cor. 4.3-4

            (2) Oppresses those who are his victims and minions through the godless world system under his control, cf. Matt. 4.1-11

            (3) Persecutes God's people through accusation, opposition, and interference, cf. Rev. 12.10

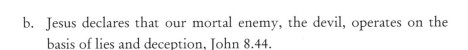

b. Jesus declares that our mortal enemy, the devil, operates on the basis of lies and deception, John 8.44.

c. The Word of God is effective in tearing down the lies and notions which have set themselves up against the knowledge of God, 2 Cor. 10.3-5.

3. Testifying to and living out God's story in the Word of God feeds and strengthens our faith, and enables us to use our weaponry effectively.

a. Defensively, we refute the devil's lies through the Word of God, through the shield of faith which extinguishes all the flaming arrows of the enemy.

(1) Eph. 6.16

(2) Rom. 10.17

b. Offensively, we are called to advance the Kingdom throughout the earth. As we declare the Word of God's story in Jesus Christ, we can frustrate our spiritual enemy and damage his enterprise through the Sword of the Spirit.

(1) Matt. 16.18

(2) Eph. 6.17

(3) 2 Tim. 3.16-17

C. God calls us to service of compassion and justice, to display the glory of Christ's Kingdom through good works and service.

1. We were created unto good works, which God has called us to do, Eph. 2.10.

2. We are a people of Christ's peculiar possession, who are zealous for good works, Titus 2.14.

3. We are to seek to do justice among all people, especially those of the household of faith, Gal. 6.9-10.

4. We are called to demonstrate the reality of our faith through loving acts of service, especially to the poor and the widow.

   a. A faith that is not accompanied by actions is an empty and dead faith, James 2.14-26.

   b. The love of God does not dwell in the heart of a person who neglects the practical need of their Christian brother, 1 John 3.16-18.

   c. True religion in the sight of God is caring for the widow and the orphan, and to keep oneself unspotted from the world, James 1.27.

   d. What we do or fail to do with the poor, the stranger, the hungry, the thirsty, the sick, the prisoner, and the naked, will be reckoned as what we did or failed to do to Jesus Christ, cf. Matt. 25.31-46.

Conclusion

» The Word that calls us to individual discipleship also calls us to live and work in Christian community, as members of his glorious family in the people of God (*laos*).

» The Word calls us to live free in Christ, loving and serving each other as we celebrate new life and use our liberty to win others for Christ.

» The Word that calls us to discipleship, community, and freedom, also calls us to mission. We have been called to fulfill the Great Commission, to do battle with our spiritual enemy the devil, and to demonstrate the life of the Kingdom through our love and good works.

Segue 2

Student Questions and Response

The following questions were designed to help you review the material in the second video segment. In understanding the nature of the Word that calls, we get a glimpse into the richness of what it means to be God's person, and to be a part of his chosen people. Be clear and concise in your answers, and where possible, support with Scripture!

1. What is the meaning of the biblical terms "regeneration" and "adoption," and how do these concepts help us to understand the nature of God's call to living in community?

2. How does the Holy Spirit, as the Spirit of adoption, help us to live and work as members of the family and people of God?

3. What are some of the major implications of suggesting the Word has called us to community? In light of these, is it possible to live out the life of discipleship and fail to be a member of a healthy body of believers? Explain your answer.

4. What does it mean that we have been called to live free in Jesus Christ? How specifically did God set us free, that is, what set us free precisely?

5. What are the elements and things from which God set us free? For what things has God set us free to do?

6. What constraints has the Lord placed on our freedom, in other words, what are the limits (if any) to the freedom that we enjoy? For what purposes have we been set free in Christ?

7. We are called to mission. What are the specific charges or tasks associated with the Church's call to engage in God's mission?

8. If Jesus has already won the battle over the devil and his minions, what exactly are we called to do as we do battle with the enemy in this world?

4

9. How does engaging in good works of service on behalf of the broken and the poor fulfill the calling of God on our lives?

This lesson focuses upon the breadth and the depth of the calling of God on the life of the person who hears and responds to the Word of God. The Word calls us to discipleship, to community, to freedom, and to engage in mission. The same Word that provides new life also calls us to life a lifestyle of radical obedience to Jesus Christ as his disciple, fulfilling our roles as ambassadors in this world.

Summary of Key Concepts

- The Word that creates new life in us through faith also calls us to live as radical disciples of Jesus Christ, serving him and his Kingdom, being obedient to his will.

- The Father calls all who believe to make themselves unconditionally available to Jesus that they might love him supremely, that they might live for him solely as Lord above all.

- We have a new identity in Christ as aliens and sojourners in this world. We are to live as Christ's ambassadors in the world, living as citizens of the Kingdom of God in the midst of an evil world, as representatives of Jesus.

- We are the servants, the bondslaves of Jesus Christ, living sacrificially to his glory. As his very own prisoners, as his servants, we are to joyfully commit all we are and have to glorifying him and accomplishing his will in the world, as he directs.

- Called to individual discipleship, we are also called to live and work in community, as members of God's glorious family in the people of God (*laos*).

- Through regeneration and adoption, the Holy Spirit has caused the new believer to share God's very own spiritual DNA, and through that, to become members of God's own family and household.

- As members of the people of God, we are called to live in the freedom of Jesus Christ, to use our freedom not as a cover for sin but as an opportunity to love others (thus fulfilling the Great Commandment), and to give clear witness for the purpose of saving others for the cause of Christ.

4

↦ The Word that calls us to discipleship, community, and freedom also calls us to mission. As witnesses of Jesus Christ, we are called to fulfill the Great Commission, to do battle with our spiritual enemy the devil, and to demonstrate the life of the Kingdom through our love and good works.

Student Application and Implications

Now is the time for you to discuss with your fellow students your questions about the calling of God through his Word on our lives. The different dimensions of discipleship, community, freedom, and mission demand constant reflection and definition, and it is critical to understand how these concepts relate to you and your life and ministry. Survey the material quickly, and determine what particular questions you now have concerning the issue of God's call. Maybe some of the questions below might help you form your own, more specific and critical questions.

* Is it possible to claim real salvation while at the same time deny Jesus as Lord in one's life? Explain your answer.

* If the call is to Christian community, what are we to do when we cannot find a church where Jesus Christ is worshiped and glorified in the way you believe he should? What about using tapes, curricula, books, and other teaching materials--can they substitute for preaching and fellowship in the Church?

* What are the enemies to living free in Christ? Isn't it dangerous to preach freedom in Jesus in our communities in the city, especially where people associate freedom with doing whatever they want to do?

* What about all the teaching today regarding "health and wealth" as the sign of God's blessing and presence? Are they all wrong? How does teaching on God's call to discipleship relate to this kind of teaching?

* Is it absolutely certain that living according to God's calling will produce suffering and persecution? Why isn't the victory that Jesus won for us automatic, that is, why didn't what Jesus did on the cross end all further struggle for us down here now?

4

In the Name of Jesus, Come out of Him

A dear sister has been diligently watching different teachers on religious television programming on the necessity and process of deliverance ministries. Completely convinced of the teaching, she has begun to teach the women in her Sunday School class that many (if not most) of the problems that believers experience and encounter are due to their neglect of casting out demons in their lives. She has begun to concentrate on this ministry, teaching techniques to release them; to identify them, to rebuke them, and claim victory over them. Some of the sisters disagree with this teaching, saying that the Apostles nowhere ask us to engage in this kind of activity. How would you handle this situation?

All Are Called to Go

In a recent missions conference at church, one of the visiting missionaries taught that, since God has called the Church to mission, everyone ought to assume that they have been called to go. If you choose to remain and not go to a field where Jesus is not known, the missionary said, you must justify your decision, because the Great Commission is to go, and it is a commission to the entire Church. Do you believe that all believers are called to go, only some are called to go, and others called to support or what?

Groovin' Hard for Jesus

In order to reach some of the gang kids in the neighborhood, the youth group has begun to sponsor some rap concert events, to draw these kids to the church. The youth group has totally embraced this vision, having repainted the youth room with "tag" art, investing some of their saved earnings in getting really nice ("nice" = really loud!) PA equipment, along with turn-tables, break-dancing, the whole works. When confronted with the worldly caste of their outreach, the youth have said, "We are using our freedom in order to save some, like Paul." What do you think of the argument they make? What should they be proud of in their position? What should they be concerned about?"

Let It Be. Let Membership Be.

 In a recent discussion among the elders about the nature of church membership, some of the elders have been arguing for the end of tight standards for membership. Most of the people come because of the solid biblical teaching, deep worship, and excellent spiritual atmosphere of the church. Only about 20% of those who attend ever come to the business meetings, which don't seem to have much to do with the church's ongoing life. Others argue that there must be a way we can tell those who are in our church apart from those who aren't, and membership standards are the easiest way to do that. What position would you take on this? How would you relate your argument to our call to live in community?

Restatement of the Lesson's Thesis

The Word that calls effectively leads us to salvation and conversion also calls us to live as disciples of Jesus, obedient to his will. It calls us to discipleship, demanding that we love Jesus supremely above all other loves as Lord above all. It asks us to embrace our new identity in Christ as aliens and sojourners in this world, living and representing Jesus as citizens of the Kingdom of God. It beckons us to live as sacrificial servants to his glory, to glorify him in all things as his Spirit leads. This Word also calls us to live and work in community, as members of God's glorious family in the people of God (*laos*). As members of his people, we are called to live in the freedom of Jesus Christ, fulfilling the Great Commandment and using it to save others for the cause of Christ. Finally, the same Word that calls to discipleship, community, and freedom also calls us to mission. As agents of the Kingdom of God, we are called to fulfill the Great Commission, to do battle with our spiritual enemy the devil, and to demonstrate the life of the Kingdom through our love and good works.

Resources and Bibliographies

If you are interested in learning more of what it means to encounter the Word of God that calls us to discipleship, community, freedom, and mission, you ought to give these books a critical read and analysis:

Phillips, Keith. *The Making of a Disciple*. Old Tappan, New Jersey: Revell, 1981.

Scott, Waldron. *Bring Forth Justice*. Grand Rapids: Eerdmans, 1980.

Snyder, Howard A. *Kingdom, Church, and World: Biblical Themes for Today*. Eugene, Oregon: Wipf and Stock Publishers, 1985.

4

Now, at the end of this module, you will be responsible to apply the insights of this course in a specific ministry activity that your mentor approves of. To really comprehend the significance of the Word's ability to transform, to convert and to call, we must use the Word practically in the context of ministry. We must share it in a situation where others can be exposed to the insights you have discovered through the course of your study. The multiple lessons to be learned through this teaching is clear: just think, for a moment, of all the practical ways that this teaching can influence your devotional life, your prayers, your response to your church, your attitude at work, and on and on and on. What is significant is that you seek to correlate this teaching with your life, work, and ministry. The ministry project is designed for this, and in the next days you will have the opportunity to share these insights in real-life, actual ministry environments. Pray that God will give you insight into his ways as you share your insights in your projects.

Ministry Connections

This final lesson on discipleship, community, freedom, and mission is full of implications for your life and ministry. Have you felt or discovered any issues, situations, or opportunities that need to be understood through the principles you learned in this lesson? What particular people has God laid upon your heart that require focused supplication and prayer for in this lesson? Take the time to ponder this, and receive the necessary support in counsel and prayer for what the Spirit has shown you.

Counseling and Prayer

4

ASSIGNMENTS

No assignment due.

Scripture Memory

No assignment due.

Reading Assignment

Your ministry project and your exegetical project should now be outlined, determined, and accepted by your instructor. Make sure that you plan ahead, so you will not be late in turning in your assignments.

Other Assignments

The final will be a take home exam, and will include questions taken from the first three quizzes, new questions on material drawn from this lesson, and essay questions which will ask for your short answer responses to key integrating

Final Exam Notice

questions. Also, you should plan on reciting or writing out the verses memorized for the course on the exam. When you have completed your exam, please notify your mentor and make certain that they get your copy.

Please note: Your module grade cannot be determined if you do not take the final exam and turn in all outstanding assignments to your mentor (ministry project, exegetical project, Scripture memory verses, reading completion sheets, quizzes, and the final exam).

The Last Word about this Module

In all the earth, there is nothing as potent and powerful as the Word of God that converts and calls, the Word regarding God's salvation to us in Jesus Christ. The Word of God is the instrument of God to equip the man or woman of God for their ministry, and if you are to be used mightily of God, you must take seriously your responsibility to become a student of the Holy Scriptures. May God give you the grace to give your heart and soul fully to mastering God's Word, so that you yourself, as well as those who hear you, may come to feel its power to create, convict, convert, and to call. Let his Word be the last word for us in this module:

Proverbs 2.1-9

[1] My son, if you receive my words
and treasure up my commandments with you,
[2] making your ear attentive to wisdom
and inclining your heart to understanding;
[3] yes, if you call out for insight
and raise your voice for understanding,
[4] if you seek it like silver
and search for it as for hidden treasures,
[5] then you will understand the fear of the Lord
and find the knowledge of God.
[6] For the Lord gives wisdom;
from his mouth come knowledge and understanding;
[7] he stores up sound wisdom for the upright;
he is a shield to those who walk in integrity,
[8] guarding the paths of justice
and watching over the way of his saints.
[9] Then you will understand righteousness and justice
and equity, every good path.

4

Appendices

APPENDIX 1

The Nicene Creed

We believe in one God,   *(Deut. 6.4-5; Mark 12.29; 1 Cor. 8.6)*
the Father Almighty,   *(Gen. 17.1; Dan. 4.35; Matt. 6.9; Eph. 4.6; Rev. 1.8)*
Maker of heaven and earth   *(Gen 1.1; Isa. 40.28; Rev. 10.6)*
and of all things visible and invisible.   *(Ps. 148; Rom. 11.36; Rev. 4.11)*

We believe in one Lord Jesus Christ, the only Begotten Son of God,
begotten of the Father before all ages,
God from God, Light from Light, True God from True God,
begotten not created,
of the same essence as the Father,   *(John 1.1-2; 3.18; 8.58; 14.9-10; 20.28; Col. 1.15, 17; Heb. 1.3-6)*
through whom all things were made.   *(John 1.3; Col. 1.16)*

Who for us men and for our salvation came down from heaven
and was incarnate by the Holy Spirit and the virgin Mary
and became human.   *(Matt. 1.20-23; John 1.14; 6.38; Luke 19.10)*
Who for us too, was crucified under Pontius Pilate,
suffered, and was buried.   *(Matt. 27.1-2; Mark 15.24-39, 43-47; Acts 13.29; Rom. 5.8; Heb. 2.10; 13.12)*
The third day he rose again
according to the Scriptures,   *(Mark 16.5-7; Luke 24.6-8; Acts 1.3; Rom. 6.9; 10.9; 2 Tim. 2.8)*
ascended into heaven,
and is seated at the right hand of the Father.   *(Mark 16.19; Eph. 1.19-20)*
He will come again in glory
to judge the living and the dead,
and his Kingdom will have no end.
(Isa. 9.7; Matt. 24.30; John 5.22; Acts 1.11; 17.31; Rom. 14.9; 2 Cor. 5.10; 2 Tim. 4.1)

We believe in the Holy Spirit, the Lord and life-giver,
(Gen. 1.1-2; Job 33.4; Ps. 104.30; 139.7-8; Luke 4.18-19; John 3.5-6; Acts 1.1-2; 1 Cor. 2.11; Rev. 3.22)
who proceeds from the Father and the Son,   *(John 14.16-18, 26; 15.26; 20.22)*
who together with the Father and Son
is worshiped and glorified,   *(Isa. 6.3; Matt. 28.19; 2 Cor. 13.14; Rev. 4.8)*
who spoke by the prophets.   *(Num. 11.29; Mic. 3.8; Acts 2.17-18; 2 Pet. 1.21)*

We believe in one holy, catholic, and apostolic Church.
(Matt. 16.18; Eph. 5.25-28; 1 Cor. 1.2; 10.17; 1 Tim. 3.15; Rev. 7.9)

We acknowledge one baptism for the forgiveness of sin,   *(Acts 22.16; 1 Pet. 3.21; Eph. 4.4-5)*
And we look for the resurrection of the dead
And the life of the age to come.   *(Isa. 11.6-10; Mic. 4.1-7; Luke 18.29-30; Rev. 21.1-5; 21.22-22.5)*

Amen.

APPENDIX 2

We Believe: Confession of the Nicene Creed (8.7.8.7. meter*)

Rev. Dr. Don L. Davis, 2007. All Rights Reserved.

* This song is adapted from the Nicene Creed, and set to 8.7.8.7. meter, meaning it can be sung to tunes of the same meter, such as: *Joyful, Joyful, We Adore Thee; I Will Sing of My Redeemer; What a Friend We Have in Jesus; Come, Thou Long Expected Jesus*

Father God Almighty rules, the Maker of both earth and heav'n.

All things seen and those unseen, by him were made, by him were giv'n!

We believe in Jesus Christ, the Lord, God's one and only Son,

Begotten, not created, too, he and our Father God are one!

Begotten from the Father, same, in essence, as both God and Light;

Through him by God all things were made, in him all things were giv'n life.

Who for us all, for our salvation, did come down from heav'n to earth,

Incarnate by the Spirit's pow'r, and through the Virgin Mary's birth.

Who for us too, was crucified, by Pontius Pilate's rule and hand,

Suffered, and was buried, yet on the third day, he rose again.

According to the Sacred Scriptures all that happ'ned was meant to be.

Ascended high to God's right hand, in heav'n he sits in glory.

Christ will come again in glory to judge all those alive and dead.

His Kingdom rule shall never end, for he will rule and reign as Head.

We worship God, the Holy Spirit, Lord and the Life-giver known;

With Fath'r and Son is glorified, Who by the prophets ever spoke.

And we believe in one true Church, God's holy people for all time,

Cath'lic in its scope and broadness, built on the Apostles' line!

Acknowledging that one baptism, for forgiv'ness of our sin,

And we look for Resurrection, for the dead shall live again.

Looking for unending days, the life of the bright Age to come,

When Christ's Reign shall come to earth, the will of God shall then be done!

Praise to God, and to Christ Jesus, to the Spirit–triune Lord!

We confess the ancient teachings, clinging to God's holy Word!

APPENDIX 3

The Story of God: Our Sacred Roots

Rev. Dr. Don L. Davis

The LORD God is the source, sustainer, and end of all things in the heavens and earth. All things were formed and exist by his will and for his eternal glory, the triune God, Father, Son, and Holy Spirit, Rom. 11.36.

	Christus Victor	Come, Holy Spirit	Your Word Is Truth	The Great Confession	His Life in Us	Living in the Way	Reborn to Serve
The Alpha and the Omega	THE TRIUNE GOD'S UNFOLDING DRAMA — God's Self-Revelation in Creation, Israel, and Christ			THE CHURCH'S PARTICIPATION IN GOD'S UNFOLDING DRAMA — Fidelity to the Apostolic Witness to Christ and His Kingdom			
	The Objective Foundation: The Sovereign Love of God — God's Narration of His Saving Work in Christ			The Subjective Practice: Salvation by Grace through Faith — The Redeemed's Joyous Response to God's Saving Work in Christ			
The Author of the Story	*The Champion of the Story*	*The Interpreter of the Story*	*The Testimony of the Story*	*The People of the Story*	*Re-enactment of the Story*	*Embodiment of the Story*	*Continuation of the Story*
The Father as Director	Jesus as Lead Actor	The Spirit as Narrator	Scripture as Script	As Saints, Confessors	As Worshipers, Ministers	As Followers, Sojourners	As Servants, Ambassadors
Christian Worldview	Communal Identity	Spiritual Experience	Biblical Authority	Orthodox Theology	Priestly Worship	Congregational Discipleship	Kingdom Witness
Theistic and Trinitarian Vision	Christ-centered Foundation	Spirit-Indwelt and -Filled Community	Canonical and Apostolic Witness	Ancient Creedal Affirmation of Faith	Weekly Gathering in Christian Assembly	Corporate, Ongoing Spiritual Formation	Active Agents of the Reign of God
Sovereign Willing	Messianic Representing	Divine Comforting	Inspired Testifying	Truthful Retelling	Joyful Excelling	Faithful Indwelling	Hopeful Compelling
Creator — True Maker of the Cosmos	Recapitulation — Typos and Fulfillment of the Covenant	Life-Giver — Regeneration and Adoption	Divine Inspiration — God-breathed Word	The Confession of Faith — Union with Christ	Song and Celebration — Historical Recitation	Pastoral Oversight — Shepherding the Flock	Explicit Unity — Love for the Saints
Owner — Sovereign Disposer of Creation	Revealer — Incarnation of the Word	Teacher — Illuminator of the Truth	Sacred History — Historical Record	Baptism into Christ — Communion of Saints	Homilies and Teachings — Prophetic Proclamation	Shared Spirituality — Common Journey through the Spiritual Disciplines	Radical Hospitality — Evidence of God's Kingdom Reign
Ruler — Blessed Controller of All Things	Redeemer — Reconciler of All Things	Helper — Endowment and the Power	Biblical Theology — Divine Commentary	The Rule of Faith — Apostles' Creed and Nicene Creed	The Lord's Supper — Dramatic Re-enactment	Embodiment — Anamnesis and Prolepsis through the Church Year	Extravagant Generosity — Good Works
Covenant Keeper — Faithful Promisor	Restorer — Christ, the Victor over the powers of evil	Guide — Divine Presence and Shekinah	Spiritual Food — Sustenance for the Journey	The Vincentian Canon — Ubiquity, antiquity, universality	Eschatological Foreshadowing — The Already/Not Yet	Effective Discipling — Spiritual Formation in the Believing Assembly	Evangelical Witness — Making Disciples of All People Groups

APPENDIX 4

The Theology of Christus Victor
A Christ-Centered Biblical Motif for Integrating and Renewing the Urban Church
Rev. Dr. Don L. Davis

	The Promised Messiah	The Word Made Flesh	The Son of Man	The Suffering Servant	The Lamb of God	The Victorious Conqueror	The Reigning Lord in Heaven	The Bridegroom and Coming King
Biblical Framework	Israel's hope of Yahweh's anointed who would redeem his people	In the person of Jesus of Nazareth, the Lord has come to the world	As the promised king and divine Son of Man, Jesus reveals the Father's glory and salvation to the world	As Inaugurator of the Kingdom of God, Jesus demonstrates God's reign present through his words, wonders, and works	As both High Priest and Paschal Lamb, Jesus offers himself to God on our behalf as a sacrifice for sin	In his resurrection from the dead and ascension to God's right hand, Jesus is proclaimed as Victor over the power of sin and death	Now reigning at God's right hand till his enemies are made his footstool, Jesus pours out his benefits on his body	Soon the risen and ascended Lord will return to gather his Bride, the Church, and consummate his work
Scripture References	Isa. 9.6-7 Jer. 23.5-6 Isa. 11.1-10	John 1.14-18 Matt. 1.20-23 Phil. 2.6-8	Matt. 2.1-11 Num. 24.17 Luke 1.78-79	Mark 1.14-15 Matt. 12.25-30 Luke 17.20-21	2 Cor. 5.18-21 Isa. 52-53 John 1.29	Eph. 1.16-23 Phil. 2.5-11 Col. 1.15-20	1 Cor. 15.25 Eph. 4.15-16 Acts. 2.32-36	Rom. 14.7-9 Rev. 5.9-13 1 Thess. 4.13-18
Jesus' History	The pre-incarnate, only begotten Son of God in glory	His conception by the Spirit, and birth to Mary	His manifestation to the Magi and to the world	His teaching, exorcisms, miracles, and mighty works among the people	His suffering, crucifixion, death, and burial	His resurrection, with appearances to his witnesses, and his ascension to the Father	The sending of the Holy Spirit and his gifts, and Christ's session in heaven at the Father's right hand	His soon return from heaven to earth as Lord and Christ: the Second Coming
Description	The biblical promise for the seed of Abraham, the prophet like Moses, the son of David	In the Incarnation, God has come to us; Jesus reveals to humankind the Father's glory in fullness	In Jesus, God has shown his salvation to the entire world, including the Gentiles	In Jesus, the promised Kingdom of God has come visibly to earth, demonstrating his binding of Satan and rescinding the Curse	As God's perfect Lamb, Jesus offers himself up to God as a sin offering on behalf of the entire world	In his resurrection and ascension, Jesus destroyed death, disarmed Satan, and rescinded the Curse	Jesus is installed at the Father's right hand as Head of the Church, Firstborn from the dead, and supreme Lord in heaven	As we labor in his harvest field in the world, so we await Christ's return, the fulfillment of his promise
Church Year	Advent	Christmas	Season after Epiphany Baptism and Transfiguration	Lent	Holy Week Passion	Eastertide Easter, Ascension Day, Pentecost	Season after Pentecost Trinity Sunday	Season after Pentecost All Saints Day, Reign of Christ the King
	The Coming of Christ	*The Birth of Christ*	*The Manifestation of Christ*	*The Ministry of Christ*	*The Suffering and Death of Christ*	*The Resurrection and Ascension of Christ*	*The Heavenly Session of Christ*	*The Reign of Christ*
Spiritual Formation	As we await his Coming, let us proclaim and affirm the hope of Christ	O Word made flesh, let us every heart prepare him room to dwell	Divine Son of Man, show the nations your salvation and glory	In the person of Christ, the power of the reign of God has come to earth and to the Church	May those who share the Lord's death be resurrected with him	Let us participate by faith in the victory of Christ over the power of sin, Satan, and death	Come, indwell us, Holy Spirit, and empower us to advance Christ's Kingdom in the world	We live and work in expectation of his soon return, seeking to please him in all things

APPENDIX 5
Christus Victor
An Integrated Vision for the Christian Life
Rev. Dr. Don L. Davis

For the Church
- The Church is the primary extension of Jesus in the world
- Ransomed treasure of the victorious, risen Christ
- *Laos:* The people of God
- God's new creation: presence of the future
- Locus and agent of the Already/Not Yet Kingdom

For Theology and Doctrine
- The authoritative Word of Christ's victory: the Apostolic Tradition: the Holy Scriptures
- Theology as commentary on the grand narrative of God
- *Christus Victor* as core theological framework for meaning in the world
- The Nicene Creed: the Story of God's triumphant grace

For Spirituality
- The Holy Spirit's presence and power in the midst of God's people
- Sharing in the disciplines of the Spirit
- Gatherings, lectionary, liturgy, and our observances in the Church Year
- Living the life of the risen Christ in the rhythm of our ordinary lives

For Gifts
- God's gracious endowments and benefits from *Christus Victor*
- Pastoral offices to the Church
- The Holy Spirit's sovereign dispensing of the gifts
- Stewardship: divine, diverse gifts for the common good

Christus Victor
Destroyer of Evil and Death
Restorer of Creation
Victor o'er Hades and Sin
Crusher of Satan

For Worship
- People of the Resurrection: unending celebration of the people of God
- Remembering, participating in the Christ event in our worship
- Listen and respond to the Word
- Transformed at the Table, the Lord's Supper
- The presence of the Father through the Son in the Spirit

For Evangelism and Mission
- Evangelism as unashamed declaration and demonstration of *Christus Victor* to the world
- The Gospel as Good News of kingdom pledge
- We proclaim God's Kingdom come in the person of Jesus of Nazareth
- The Great Commission: go to all people groups making disciples of Christ and his Kingdom
- Proclaiming Christ as Lord and Messiah

For Justice and Compassion
- The gracious and generous expressions of Jesus through the Church
- The Church displays the very life of the Kingdom
- The Church demonstrates the very life of the Kingdom of heaven right here and now
- Having freely received, we freely give (no sense of merit or pride)
- Justice as tangible evidence of the Kingdom come

APPENDIX 6

Old Testament Witness to Christ and His Kingdom

Rev. Dr. Don L. Davis

Christ Is Seen in the OT's:	Covenant Promise and Fulfillment	Moral Law	Christophanies	Typology	Tabernacle, Festival, and Levitical Priesthood	Messianic Prophecy	Salvation Promises
Passage	Gen. 12.1-3	Matt. 5.17-18	John 1.18	1 Cor. 15.45	Heb. 8.1-6	Mic. 5.2	Isa. 9.6-7
Example	The Promised Seed of the Abrahamic covenant	The Law given on Mount Sinai	Commander of the Lord's army	Jonah and the great fish	Melchizedek, as both High Priest and King	The Lord's Suffering Servant	Righteous Branch of David
Christ As	Seed of the woman	The Prophet of God	God's present Revelation	Antitype of God's drama	Our eternal High Priest	The coming Son of Man	Israel's Redeemer and King
Where Illustrated	Galatians	Matthew	John	Matthew	Hebrews	Luke and Acts	John and Revelation
Exegetical Goal	To see Christ as heart of God's sacred drama	To see Christ as fulfillment of the Law	To see Christ as God's revealer	To see Christ as antitype of divine typos	To see Christ in the Temple *cultus*	To see Christ as true Messiah	To see Christ as coming King
How Seen in the NT	As fulfillment of God's sacred oath	As *telos* of the Law	As full, final, and superior revelation	As substance behind the historical shadows	As reality behind the rules and roles	As the Kingdom made present	As the One who will rule on David's throne
Our Response in Worship	God's veracity and faithfulness	God's perfect righteousness	God's presence among us	God's inspired Scripture	God's ontology: his realm as primary and determinative	God's anointed servant and mediator	God's resolve to restore his kingdom authority
How God Is Vindicated	God does not lie: he's true to his word	Jesus fulfills all righteousness	God's fulness is revealed to us in Jesus of Nazareth	The Spirit spoke by the prophets	The Lord has provided a mediator for humankind	Every jot and tittle written of him will occur	Evil will be put down, creation restored, under his reign

APPENDIX 7

Summary Outline of the Scriptures

Rev. Dr. Don L. Davis

1. GENESIS - Beginnings
   a. Adam
   b. Noah
   c. Abraham
   d. Isaac
   e. Jacob
   f. Joseph

2. EXODUS - Redemption, (out of)
   a. Slavery
   b. Deliverance
   c. Law
   d. Tabernacle

3. LEVITICUS - Worship and Fellowship
   a. Offerings, sacrifices
   b. Priests
   c. Feasts, festivals

4. NUMBERS - Service and Walk
   a. Organized
   b. Wanderings

5. DEUTERONOMY - Obedience
   a. Moses reviews history and law
   b. Civil and social laws
   c. Palestinian Covenant
   d. Moses' blessing and death

6. JOSHUA - Redemption (into)
   a. Conquer the land
   b. Divide up the land
   c. Joshua's farewell

7. JUDGES - God's Deliverance
   a. Disobedience and judgment
   b. Israel's twelve judges
   c. Lawless conditions

8. RUTH - Love
   a. Ruth chooses
   b. Ruth works
   c. Ruth waits
   d. Ruth rewarded

9. 1 SAMUEL - Kings, Priestly Perspective
   a. Eli
   b. Samuel
   c. Saul
   d. David

10. 2 SAMUEL - David
    a. King of Judah
       (9 years - Hebron)
    b. King of all Israel
       (33 years - Jerusalem)

11. 1 KINGS - Solomon's Glory, Kingdom's Decline
    a. Solomon's glory
    b. Kingdom's decline
    c. Elijah the prophet

12. 2 KINGS- Divided Kingdom
    a. Elisha
    b. Israel (N. Kingdom falls)
    c. Judah (S. Kingdom falls)

13. 1 CHRONICLES - David's Temple Arrangements
    a. Genealogies
    b. End of Saul's reign
    c. Reign of David
    d. Temple preparations

14. 2 CHRONICLES - Temple and Worship Abandoned
    a. Solomon
    b. Kings of Judah

15. EZRA - The Minority (Remnant)
    a. First return from exile - Zerubbabel
    b. Second return from exile - Ezra (priest)

16. NEHEMIAH - Rebuilding by Faith
    a. Rebuild walls
    b. Revival
    c. Religious reform

17. ESTHER - Female Savior
    a. Esther
    b. Haman
    c. Mordecai
    d. Deliverance: Feast of Purim

18. JOB - Why the Righteous Suffer
    a. Godly Job
    b. Satan's attack
    c. Four philosophical friends
    d. God lives

19. PSALMS - Prayer and Praise
    a. Prayers of David
    b. Godly suffer; deliverance
    c. God deals with Israel
    d. Suffering of God's people - end with the Lord's reign
    e. The Word of God (Messiah's suffering and glorious return)

20. PROVERBS - Wisdom
    a. Wisdom versus folly
    b. Solomon
    c. Solomon - Hezekiah
    d. Agur
    e. Lemuel

21. ECCLESIASTES - Vanity
    a. Experimentation
    b. Observation
    c. Consideration

22. SONG OF SOLOMON - Love Story

23. ISAIAH - The Justice (Judgment) and Grace (Comfort) of God
    a. Prophecies of punishment
    b. History
    c. Prophecies of blessing

24. JEREMIAH - Judah's Sin Leads to Babylonian Captivity
    a. Jeremiah's call; empowered
    b. Judah condemned; predicted Babylonian captivity
    c. Restoration promised
    d. Prophesied judgment inflicted
    e. Prophesies against Gentiles
    f. Summary of Judah's captivity

25. LAMENTATIONS - Lament over Jerusalem
    a. Affliction of Jerusalem
    b. Destroyed because of sin
    c. The prophet's suffering
    d. Present desolation versus past splendor
    e. Appeal to God for mercy

26. EZEKIEL - Israel's Captivity and Restoration
    a. Judgment on Judah and Jerusalem
    b. Judgment on Gentile nations
    c. Israel restored; Jerusalem's future glory

27. DANIEL - The Time of the Gentiles
    a. History; Nebuchadnezzar, Belshazzar, Daniel
    b. Prophecy

28. HOSEA - Unfaithfulness
    a. Unfaithfulness
    b. Punishment
    c. Restoration

29. JOEL - The Day of the Lord
    a. Locust plague
    b. Events of the future day of the Lord
    c. Order of the future day of the Lord

30. AMOS - God Judges Sin
    a. Neighbors judged
    b. Israel judged
    c. Visions of future judgment
    d. Israel's past judgment blessings

31. OBADIAH - Edom's Destruction
    a. Destruction prophesied
    b. Reasons for destruction
    c. Israel's future blessing

32. JONAH - Gentile Salvation
    a. Jonah disobeys
    b. Other suffer
    c. Jonah punished
    d. Jonah obeys; thousands saved
    e. Jonah displeased, no love for souls

33. MICAH - Israel's Sins, Judgment, and Restoration
    a. Sin and judgment
    b. Grace and future restoration
    c. Appeal and petition

34. NAHUM - Nineveh Condemned
    a. God hates sin
    b. Nineveh's doom prophesied
    c. Reasons for doom

35. HABAKKUK - The Just Shall Live by Faith
    a. Complaint of Judah's unjudged sin
    b. Chaldeans will punish
    c. Complaint of Chaldeans' wickedness
    d. Punishment promised
    e. Prayer for revival; faith in God

36. ZEPHANIAH - Babylonian Invasion Prefigures the Day of the Lord
    a. Judgment on Judah foreshadows the Great Day of the Lord
    b. Judgment on Jerusalem and neighbors foreshadows final judgment of all nations
    c. Israel restored after judgments

37. HAGGAI - Rebuild the Temple
    a. Negligence
    b. Courage
    c. Separation
    d. Judgment

38. ZECHARIAH - Two Comings of Christ
    a. Zechariah's vision
    b. Bethel's question; Jehovah's answer
    c. Nation's downfall and salvation

39. MALACHI - Neglect
    a. The priest's sins
    b. The people's sins
    c. The faithful few

Summary Outline of the Scriptures (continued)

1. MATTHEW - Jesus the King
  a. The Person of the King
  b. The Preparation of the King
  c. The Propaganda of the King
  d. The Program of the King
  e. The Passion of the King
  f. The Power of the King
	7. 1 CORINTHIANS - The Lordship of Christ
	  a. Salutation and thanksgiving
	  b. Conditions in the Corinthian body
	  c. Concerning the Gospel
	  d. Concerning collections
		14. 2 THESSALONIANS - The Second Coming of Christ
		  a. Persecution of believers now; judgment of unbelievers hereafter (at coming of Christ)
		  b. Program of the world in connection with the coming of Christ
		  c. Practical issues associated with the coming of Christ
			21. 1 PETER - Christian Hope in the Time of Persecution and Trial
			  a. Suffering and security of believers
			  b. Suffering and the Scriptures
			  c. Suffering and the sufferings of Christ
			  d. Suffering and the Second Coming of Christ

2. MARK - Jesus the Servant
  a. John introduces the Servant
  b. God the Father identifies the Servant
  c. The temptation initiates the Servant
  d. Work and word of the Servant
  e. Death, burial, resurrection
	8. 2 CORINTHIANS - The Ministry in the Church
	  a. The comfort of God
	  b. Collection for the poor
	  c. Calling of the Apostle Paul
		15. 1 TIMOTHY - Government and Order in the Local Church
		  a. The faith of the Church
		  b. Public prayer and women's place in the Church
		  c. Officers in the Church
		  d. Apostasy in the Church
		  e. Duties of the officer of the Church
			22. 2 PETER - Warning Against False Teachers
			  a. Addition of Christian graces gives assurance
			  b. Authority of the Scriptures
			  c. Apostasy brought in by false testimony
			  d. Attitude toward Return of Christ: test for apostasy
			  e. Agenda of God in the world
			  f. Admonition to believers

3. LUKE - Jesus Christ the Perfect Man
  a. Birth and family of the Perfect Man
  b. Testing of the Perfect Man; hometown
  c. Ministry of the Perfect Man
  d. Betrayal, trial, and death of the Perfect Man
  e. Resurrection of the Perfect Man
	9. GALATIANS - Justification by Faith
	  a. Introduction
	  b. Personal - Authority of the Apostle and glory of the Gospel
	  c. Doctrinal - Justification by faith
	  d. Practical - Sanctification by the Holy Spirit
	  e. Autographed conclusion and exhortation
		16. 2 TIMOTHY - Loyalty in the Days of Apostasy
		  a. Afflictions of the Gospel
		  b. Active in service
		  c. Apostasy coming; authority of the Scriptures
		  d. Allegiance to the Lord
			23. 1 JOHN - The Family of God
			  a. God is Light
			  b. God is Love
			  c. God is Life

4. JOHN - Jesus Christ is God
  a. Prologue - the Incarnation
  b. Introduction
  c. Witness of Jesus to his Apostles
  d. Passion - witness to the world
  e. Epilogue
	10. EPHESIANS - The Church of Jesus Christ
	  a. Doctrinal - the heavenly calling of the Church
	    A Body
	    A Temple
	    A Mystery
	  b. Practical - The earthly conduct of the Church
	    A New Man
	    A Bride
	    An Army
		17. TITUS - The Ideal New Testament Church
		  a. The Church is an organization
		  b. The Church is to teach and preach the Word of God
		  c. The Church is to perform good works
			24. 2 JOHN - Warning against Receiving Deceivers
			  a. Walk in truth
			  b. Love one another
			  c. Receive not deceivers
			  d. Find joy in fellowship

5. ACTS - The Holy Spirit Working in the Church
  a. The Lord Jesus at work by the Holy Spirit through the Apostles at Jerusalem
  b. In Judea and Samaria
  c. To the uttermost parts of the Earth
	11. PHILIPPIANS - Joy in the Christian Life
	  a. Philosophy for Christian living
	  b. Pattern for Christian living
	  c. Prize for Christian living
	  d. Power for Christian living
		18. PHILEMON - Reveal Christ's Love and Teach Brotherly Love
		  a. Genial greeting to Philemon and family
		  b. Good reputation of Philemon
		  c. Gracious plea for Onesimus
		  d. Guiltless illustration of Imputation
		  e. General and personal requests
			25. 3 JOHN - Admonition to Receive True Believers
			  a. Gaius, brother in the Church
			  b. Diotrephes
			  c. Demetrius

6. ROMANS - The Righteousness of God
  a. Salutation
  b. Sin and salvation
  c. Sanctification
  d. Struggle
  e. Spirit-filled living
  f. Security of salvation
  g. Segregation
  h. Sacrifice and service
  i. Separation and salutation
	12. COLOSSIANS - Christ the Fullness of God
	  a. Doctrinal - In Christ believers are made full
	  b. Practical - Christ's life poured out in believers, and through them
	
	13. 1 THESSALONIANS - The Second Coming of Christ:
	  a. Is an inspiring hope
	  b. Is a working hope
	  c. Is a purifying hope
	  d. Is a comforting hope
	  e. Is a rousing, stimulating hope
		19. HEBREWS - The Superiority of Christ
		  a. Doctrinal - Christ is better than the Old Testament economy
		  b. Practical - Christ brings better benefits and duties
		
		20. JAMES - Ethics of Christianity
		  a. Faith tested
		  b. Difficulty of controlling the tongue
		  c. Warning against worldliness
		  d. Admonitions in view of the Lord's coming
			26. JUDE - Contending for the Faith
			  a. Occasion of the epistle
			  b. Occurrences of apostasy
			  c. Occupation of believers in the days of apostasy
			
			27. REVELATION - The Unveiling of Christ Glorified
			  a. The person of Christ in glory
			  b. The possession of Jesus Christ - the Church in the World
			  c. The program of Jesus Christ - the scene in Heaven
			  d. The seven seals
			  e. The seven trumpets
			  f. Important persons in the last days
			  g. The seven vials
			  h. The fall of Babylon
			  i. The eternal state

A P P E N D I X   8

From Before to Beyond Time:

The Plan of God and Human History

Adapted from Suzanne de Dietrich. **God's Unfolding Purpose.** *Philadelphia: Westminster Press, 1976.*

I. Before Time (Eternity Past) 1 Cor. 2.7
   A. The Eternal Triune God
   B. God's Eternal Purpose
   C. The Mystery of Iniquity
   D. The Principalities and Powers

II. Beginning of Time (Creation and Fall) Gen. 1.1
   A. Creative Word
   B. Humanity
   C. Fall
   D. Reign of Death and First Signs of Grace

III. Unfolding of Time (God's Plan Revealed Through Israel) Gal. 3.8
   A. Promise (Patriarchs)
   B. Exodus and Covenant at Sinai
   C. Promised Land
   D. The City, the Temple, and the Throne (Prophet, Priest, and King)
   E. Exile
   F. Remnant

IV. Fullness of Time (Incarnation of the Messiah) Gal. 4.4-5
   A. The King Comes to His Kingdom
   B. The Present Reality of His Reign
   C. The Secret of the Kingdom: the Already and the Not Yet
   D. The Crucified King
   E. The Risen Lord

V. The Last Times (The Descent of the Holy Spirit) Acts 2.16-18
   A. Between the Times: the Church as Foretaste of the Kingdom
   B. The Church as Agent of the Kingdom
   C. The Conflict Between the Kingdoms of Darkness and Light

VI. The Fulfillment of Time (The Second Coming) Matt. 13.40-43
   A. The Return of Christ
   B. Judgment
   C. The Consummation of His Kingdom

VII. Beyond Time (Eternity Future) 1 Cor. 15.24-28
   A. Kingdom Handed Over to God the Father
   B. God as All in All

From Before to Beyond Time
Scriptures for Major Outline Points

I. Before Time (Eternity Past)

1 Cor. 2.7 (ESV) - But we impart a secret and hidden wisdom of God, *which God decreed before the ages* for our glory (cf. Titus 1.2).

II. Beginning of Time (Creation and Fall)

Gen. 1.1 (ESV) - *In the beginning*, God created the heavens and the earth.

III. Unfolding of Time (God's Plan Revealed Through Israel)

Gal. 3.8 (ESV) - And the Scripture, foreseeing that God would justify the Gentiles by faith, *preached the Gospel beforehand to Abraham*, saying, "In you shall all the nations be blessed" (cf. Rom. 9.4-5).

IV. Fullness of Time (The Incarnation of the Messiah)

Gal. 4.4-5 (ESV) - *But when the fullness of time had come*, God sent forth his Son, born of woman, born under the law, to redeem those who were under the law, so that we might receive adoption as sons.

V. The Last Times (The Descent of the Holy Spirit)

Acts 2.16-18 (ESV) - But this is what was uttered through the prophet Joel: "'*And in the last days it shall be*,' God declares, 'that I will pour out my Spirit on all flesh, and your sons and your daughters shall prophesy, and your young men shall see visions, and your old men shall dream dreams; even on my male servants and female servants in those days I will pour out my Spirit, and they shall prophesy.'"

VI. The Fulfillment of Time (The Second Coming)

Matt. 13.40-43 (ESV) - Just as the weeds are gathered and burned with fire, *so will it be at the close of the age*. The Son of Man will send his angels, and they will gather out of his Kingdom all causes of sin and all lawbreakers, and throw them into the fiery furnace. In that place there will be weeping and gnashing of teeth. Then the righteous will shine like the sun in the Kingdom of their Father. He who has ears, let him hear.

VII. Beyond Time (Eternity Future)

1 Cor. 15.24-28 (ESV) - Then comes the end, when he delivers the Kingdom to God the Father after destroying every rule and every authority and power. For he must reign until he has put all his enemies under his feet. The last enemy to be destroyed is death. For "God has put all things in subjection under his feet." But when it says, "all things are put in subjection," it is plain that he is excepted who put all things in subjection under him. When all things are subjected to him, then the Son himself will also be subjected to him who put all things in subjection under him, that God may be all in all.

APPENDIX 9

"There Is a River"

Identifying the Streams of a Revitalized Authentic Christian Community in the City[1]

Rev. Dr. Don L. Davis • Psalm 46.4 (ESV) - There is a river whose streams make glad the city of God, the holy habitation of the Most High.

Tributaries of Authentic Historic Biblical Faith			
Recognized **Biblical Identity**	*Revived* **Urban Spirituality**	*Reaffirmed* **Historical Connectivity**	*Refocused* **Kingdom Authority**
The Church Is **One**	The Church Is **Holy**	The Church Is **Catholic**	The Church Is **Apostolic**
A Call to Biblical Fidelity *Recognizing the Scriptures as the anchor and foundation of the Christian faith and practice*	**A Call to the Freedom, Power, and Fullness of the Holy Spirit** *Walking in the holiness, power, gifting, and liberty of the Holy Spirit in the body of Christ*	**A Call to Historic Roots and Continuity** *Confessing the common historical identity and continuity of authentic Christian faith*	**A Call to the Apostolic Faith** *Affirming the apostolic tradition as the authoritative ground of the Christian hope*
A Call to Messianic Kingdom Identity *Rediscovering the story of the promised Messiah and his Kingdom in Jesus of Nazareth*	**A Call to Live as Sojourners and Aliens as the People of God** *Defining authentic Christian discipleship as faithful membership among God's people*	**A Call to Affirm and Express the Global Communion of Saints** *Expressing cooperation and collaboration with all other believers, both local and global*	**A Call to Representative Authority** *Submitting joyfully to God's gifted servants in the Church as undershepherds of true faith*
A Call to Creedal Affinity *Embracing the Nicene Creed as the shared rule of faith of historic orthodoxy*	**A Call to Liturgical, Sacramental, and Catechetical Vitality** *Experiencing God's presence in the context of the Word, sacrament, and instruction*	**A Call to Radical Hospitality and Good Works** *Expressing kingdom love to all, and especially to those of the household of faith*	**A Call to Prophetic and Holistic Witness** *Proclaiming Christ and his Kingdom in word and deed to our neighbors and all peoples*

[1] *This schema is an adaptation and is based on the insights of the* **Chicago Call** *statement of May 1977, where various leading evangelical scholars and practitioners met to discuss the relationship of modern evangelicalism to the historic Christian faith.*

APPENDIX 10
A Schematic for a Theology of the Kingdom and the Church
The Urban Ministry Institute

The Reign of the One, True, Sovereign, and Triune God, the LORD God, Yahweh, God the Father, Son, and Holy Spirit

The Father	The Son	The Spirit
The Father Love - 1 John 4.8 Maker of heaven and earth and of all things visible and invisible	**The Son** Faith - Heb. 12.2 Prophet, Priest, and King	**The Spirit** Hope - Rom. 15.13 Lord of the Church
Creation All that exists through the creative action of God.	**Kingdom** The Reign of God expressed in the rule of his Son Jesus the Messiah.	**Church** The one, holy, apostolic community which functions as a witness to (Acts 28.31) and a foretaste of (Col. 1.12; James 1.18; 1 Pet. 2.9; Rev. 1.6) the Kingdom of God.

The eternal God, sovereign in power, infinite in wisdom, perfect in holiness, and steadfast in love, is the source and goal of all things.

Rom. 8.18-21 →

O, the depth of the riches and wisdom and knowledge of God! How unsearchable are his judgments, and how inscrutable his ways! For who has known the mind of the Lord, or who has been his counselor? Or who has ever given a gift to him, that he might be repaid?' For from him and through him and to him are all things. To him be glory forever! Amen! - Rom. 11.33-36 (ESV) (cf. 1 Cor. 15.23-28; Rev.)

Rev. 21.1-5 →

Isa. 11.6-9 →

The Son

Freedom (Slavery)

Jesus answered them, "Truly, truly, I say to you, everyone who commits sin is a slave to sin. The slave does not remain in the house forever; the son remains forever. So if the Son sets you free, you will be free indeed." - John 8.34-36 (ESV)

Wholeness (Sickness)

But he was wounded for our transgressions; he was crushed for our iniquities; upon him was the chastisement that brought us peace, and with his stripes we are healed. - Isa. 53.5 (ESV)

Justice (Selfishness)

Behold, my servant whom I have chosen, my beloved with whom my soul is well pleased. I will put my Spirit upon him, and he will proclaim justice to the Gentiles. He will not quarrel or cry aloud, nor will anyone hear his voice in the streets; a bruised reed he will not break, and a smoldering wick he will not quench, until he brings justice to victory. - Matt. 12.18-20 (ESV)

The Spirit / Church

The Church is an Apostolic Community Where the Word is Rightly Preached, Therefore it is a Community of:

Calling - For freedom Christ has set us free; stand firm therefore, and do not submit again to a yoke of slavery. - Gal. 5.1 (ESV) (cf. Rom. 8.28-30; 1 Cor. 1.26-31; Eph. 1.18; 2 Thess. 2.13-14; Jude 1.1)

Faith - "... for unless you believe that I am he you will die in your sins" . . . So Jesus said to the Jews who had believed in him, "If you abide in my word, you are truly my disciples, and you will know the truth, and the truth will set you free." - John 8.24b, 31-32 (ESV) (cf. Ps. 119.45; Rom. 1.17; 5.1-2; Eph. 2.8-9; 2 Tim. 1.13-14; Heb. 2.14-15; James 1.25)

Witness - The Spirit of the Lord is upon me, because he has anointed me to proclaim good news to the poor. He has sent me to proclaim liberty to the captives and recovering of sight to the blind, to set at liberty those who are oppressed, to proclaim the year of the Lord's favor. - Luke 4.18-19 (ESV) (cf. Lev. 25.10; Prov. 31.8; Matt. 4.17; 28.18-20; Mark 13.10; Acts 1.8; 8.4, 12; 13.1-3; 25.20; 28.30-31)

The Church is One Community Where the Sacraments are Rightly Administered, Therefore it is a Community of:

Worship - You shall serve the Lord your God, and he will bless your bread and your water, and I will take sickness away from among you. - Exod. 23.25 (ESV) (cf. Ps. 147.1-3; Heb. 12.28; Col. 3.16; Rev. 15.3-4; 19.5)

Covenant - And the Holy Spirit also bears witness to us; for after the saying, "This is the covenant that I will make with them after those days, declares the Lord: I will put my laws on their hearts, and write them on their minds," then he adds, "I will remember their sins and their lawless deeds no more." - Heb. 10.15-17 (ESV) (cf. Isa. 54.10-17; Ezek. 34.25-31; 37.26-27; Mal. 2.4-5; Luke 22.20; 2 Cor. 3.6; Col. 3.15; Heb. 8.7-13; 12.22-24; 13.20-21)

Presence - In him you also are being built together into a dwelling place for God by his Spirit. - Eph. 2.22 (ESV) (cf. Exod. 40.34-38; Ezek. 48.35; Matt. 18.18-20)

The Church is a Holy Community Where Discipline is Rightly Ordered, Therefore it is a Community of:

Reconciliation - For he himself is our peace, who has made us both one and has broken down in his flesh the dividing wall of hostility by abolishing the law of commandments and ordinances, that he might create in himself one new man in place of the two, so making peace, and might reconcile us both to God in one body through the cross, thereby killing the hostility. And he came and preached peace to you who were far off and peace to those who were near. For through him we both have access in one Spirit to the Father. - Eph. 2.14-18 (ESV) (cf. Exod. 23.4-9; Lev. 19.34; Deut. 10.18-19; Ezek. 22.29; Mic. 6.8; 2 Cor. 5.16-21)

Suffering - Since therefore Christ suffered in the flesh, arm yourselves with the same way of thinking, for whoever has suffered in the flesh has ceased from sin, so as to live for the rest of the time in the flesh no longer for human passions but for the will of God. - 1 Pet. 4.1-2 (ESV) (cf. Luke 6.22; 10.3; Rom. 8.17; 2 Tim. 2.3; 3.12; 1 Pet. 2.20-24; Heb. 5.8; 13.11-14)

Service - But Jesus called them to him and said, "You know that the rulers of the Gentiles lord it over them, and their great ones exercise authority over them. It shall not be so among you. But whoever would be great among you must be your servant, and whoever would be first among you must be your slave even as the Son of Man came not to be served but to serve, and to give his life as a ransom for many." - Matt. 20.25-28 (ESV) (cf. 1 John 4.16-18; Gal. 2.10)

APPENDIX 11
Living in the Already and the Not Yet Kingdom
Rev. Dr. Don L. Davis

The Spirit: The pledge of the inheritance (***arrabon***)
The Church: The foretaste (***aparche***) of the Kingdom
"In Christ": The rich life (***en Christos***) we share as citizens of the Kingdom

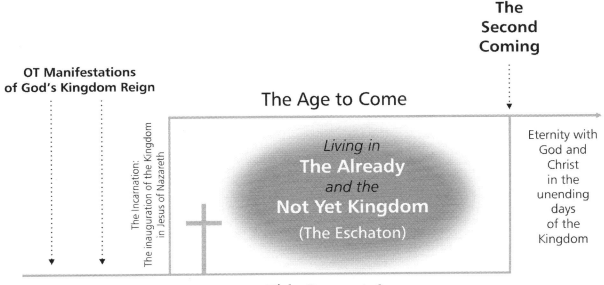

Internal enemy: The flesh (*sarx*) and the sin nature
External enemy: The world (*kosmos*) the systems of greed, lust, and pride
Infernal enemy: The devil (*kakos*) the animating spirit of falsehood and fear

Jewish View of Time

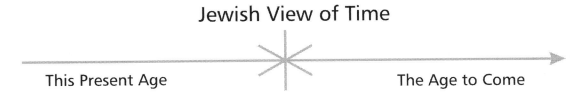

This Present Age   The Age to Come

The Coming of Messiah
The restoration of Israel
The end of Gentile oppression
The return of the earth to Edenic glory
Universal knowledge of the Lord

APPENDIX 12

Jesus of Nazareth: The Presence of the Future

Rev. Dr. Don L. Davis

Glorification: New Heavens and New Earth

Consummation

Creation: The Reign of Almighty God

The Cross:
The Center of Revelation and Redemption

The Spirit of God   "The Age of the Spirit"

Church

Between the Times

The Church

Sign and Foretaste
Prophetic Witness
The Promise Fulfilled

The Incarnation
"The Kingdom is at hand!"
Invasion of Satan's Dominion
Rescinding of the Curse
Emblems of the Age to Come
Promise of the Holy Spirit
Defeat of the Powers and Principalities

Covenant

The Divine Promise

Abraham
Isaac
Jacob
Judah
David

Creation

The Fall

Curse (Death)

Slavery
Selfishness
Sickness

APPENDIX 13

Traditions

(Paradosis)

Dr. Don L. Davis and Rev. Terry G. Cornett

Strong's Definition

Paradosis. Transmission, i.e. (concretely) a precept; specifically, the Jewish traditionary law

Vine's Explanation

denotes "a tradition," and hence, by metonymy, (a) "the teachings of the rabbis," . . . (b) "apostolic teaching," . . . of instructions concerning the gatherings of believers, of Christian doctrine in general . . . of instructions concerning everyday conduct.

1. **The concept of tradition in Scripture is essentially positive.**

   Jer. 6.16 (ESV) - Thus says the Lord: "Stand by the roads, and look, and ask for the ancient paths, where the good way is; and walk in it, and find rest for your souls. But they said, 'We will not walk in it'" (cf. Exod. 3.15; Judg. 2.17; 1 Kings 8.57-58; Ps. 78.1-6).

   2 Chron. 35.25 (ESV) - Jeremiah also uttered a lament for Josiah; and all the singing men and singing women have spoken of Josiah in their laments to this day. They made these a rule in Israel; behold, they are written in the Laments (cf. Gen. 32.32; Judg. 11.38-40).

   Jer. 35.14-19 (ESV) - The command that Jonadab the son of Rechab gave to his sons, to drink no wine, has been kept, and they drink none to this day, for they have obeyed their father's command. I have spoken to you persistently, but you have not listened to me. I have sent to you all my servants the prophets, sending them persistently, saying, 'Turn now every one of you from his evil way, and amend your deeds, and do not go after other gods to serve them, and then you shall dwell in the land that I gave to you and your fathers.' But you did not incline your ear or listen to me. The sons of Jonadab the son of Rechab have kept the command that their father gave them, but this people has not obeyed me. Therefore, thus says the

Traditions (continued)

Lord, the God of hosts, the God of Israel: Behold, I am bringing upon Judah and all the inhabitants of Jerusalem all the disaster that I have pronounced against them, because I have spoken to them and they have not listened, I have called to them and they have not answered." But to the house of the Rechabites Jeremiah said, "Thus says the Lord of hosts, the God of Israel: Because you have obeyed the command of Jonadab your father and kept all his precepts and done all that he commanded you, therefore thus says the Lord of hosts, the God of Israel: Jonadab the son of Rechab shall never lack a man to stand before me."

2. Godly tradition is a wonderful thing, but not all tradition is godly.

Any individual tradition must be judged by its faithfulness to the Word of God and its usefulness in helping people maintain obedience to Christ's example and teaching.[1] In the Gospels, Jesus frequently rebukes the Pharisees for establishing traditions that nullify rather than uphold God's commands.

Mark 7.8 (ESV) - You leave the commandment of God and hold to the tradition of men" (cf. Matt. 15.2-6; Mark 7.13).

Col. 2.8 (ESV) - See to it that no one takes you captive by philosophy and empty deceit, according to human tradition, according to the elemental spirits of the world, and not according to Christ.

3. Without the fullness of the Holy Spirit, and the constant edification provided to us by the Word of God, tradition will inevitably lead to dead formalism.

Those who are spiritual are filled with the Holy Spirit, whose power and leading alone provides individuals and congregations a sense of freedom and vitality in all they practice and believe. However, when the practices and teachings of any given tradition are no longer infused by the power of the Holy Spirit and the Word of God, tradition loses its effectiveness, and may actually become counterproductive to our discipleship in Jesus Christ.

Eph. 5.18 (ESV) - And do not get drunk with wine, for that is debauchery, but be filled with the Spirit.

[1] "All Protestants insist that these traditions must ever be tested against Scripture and can never possess an independent apostolic authority over or alongside of Scripture." (J. Van Engen, "Tradition," *Evangelical Dictionary of Theology,* Walter Elwell, Gen. ed.) We would add that Scripture is itself the "authoritative tradition" by which all other traditions are judged. See "Appendix A, The Founders of Tradition: Three Levels of Christian Authority," p. 4.

Gal. 5.22-25 (ESV) - But the fruit of the Spirit is love, joy, peace, patience, kindness, goodness, faithfulness, gentleness, self-control; against such things there is no law. And those who belong to Christ Jesus have crucified the flesh with its passions and desires. If we live by the Spirit, let us also walk by the Spirit.

2 Cor. 3.5-6 (ESV) - Not that we are sufficient in ourselves to claim anything as coming from us, but our sufficiency is from God, who has made us competent to be ministers of a new covenant, not of the letter but of the Spirit. For the letter kills, but the Spirit gives life.

4. **Fidelity to the Apostolic Tradition (teaching and modeling) is the essence of Christian maturity.**

2 Tim. 2.2 (ESV) - and what you have heard from me in the presence of many witnesses entrust to faithful men who will be able to teach others also.

1 Cor. 11.1-2 (ESV) - Be imitators of me, as I am of Christ. Now I commend you because you remember me in everything and maintain the traditions even as I delivered them to you (cf.1 Cor. 4.16-17, 2 Tim. 1.13-14, 2 Thess. 3.7-9, Phil. 4.9).

1 Cor. 15.3-8 (ESV) - For I delivered to you as of first importance what I also received: that Christ died for our sins in accordance with the Scriptures, that he was buried, that he was raised on the third day in accordance with the Scriptures, and that he appeared to Cephas, then to the twelve. Then he appeared to more than five hundred brothers at one time, most of whom are still alive, though some have fallen asleep. Then he appeared to James, then to all the apostles. Last of all, as to one untimely born, he appeared also to me.

5. **The Apostle Paul often includes an appeal to the tradition for support in doctrinal practices.**

1 Cor. 11.16 (ESV) - If anyone is inclined to be contentious, we have no such practice, nor do the churches of God (cf. 1 Cor. 1.2, 7.17, 15.3).

Traditions (continued)

1 Cor. 14.33-34 (ESV) - For God is not a God of confusion but of peace. As in all the churches of the saints, the women should keep silent in the churches. For they are not permitted to speak, but should be in submission, as the Law also says.

6. When a congregation uses received tradition to remain faithful to the "Word of God," they are commended by the apostles.

1 Cor. 11.2 (ESV) - Now I commend you because you remember me in everything and maintain the traditions even as I delivered them to you.

2 Thess. 2.15 (ESV) - So then, brothers, stand firm and hold to the traditions that you were taught by us, either by our spoken word or by our letter.

2 Thess. 3.6 (ESV) - Now we command you, brothers, in the name of our Lord Jesus Christ, that you keep away from any brother who is walking in idleness and not in accord with the tradition that you received from us.

Appendix A

The Founders of Tradition: Three Levels of Christian Authority

Exod. 3.15 (ESV) - God also said to Moses, "Say this to the people of Israel, 'The Lord, the God of your fathers, the God of Abraham, the God of Isaac, and the God of Jacob, has sent me to you.' This is my name forever, and thus I am to be remembered throughout all generations."

1. The Authoritative Tradition: the Apostles and the Prophets (The Holy Scriptures)

Eph. 2.19-21 (ESV) - So then you are no longer strangers and aliens, but you are fellow citizens with the saints and members of the household of God, built on the foundation of the apostles and prophets, Christ Jesus himself being the cornerstone, in whom the whole structure, being joined together, grows into a holy temple in the Lord.

~ The Apostle Paul

Those who gave eyewitness testimony to the revelation and saving acts of Yahweh, first in Israel, and ultimately in Jesus Christ the Messiah. This testimony is binding for all people, at all times, and in all places. It is the authoritative tradition by which all subsequent tradition is judged.

2. The Great Tradition: the Ecumenical Councils and their Creeds[2]

What has been believed everywhere, always, and by all.

~ Vincent of Lerins

The Great Tradition is the core dogma (doctrine) of the Church. It represents the teaching of the Church as it has understood the Authoritative Tradition (the Holy Scriptures), and summarizes those essential truths that Christians of all ages have confessed and believed. To these doctrinal statements the whole Church, (Catholic, Orthodox, and Protestant)[3] gives its assent. The worship and theology of the Church reflects this core dogma, which finds its summation and fulfillment in the person and work of Jesus Christ. From earliest times, Christians have expressed their devotion to God in its Church calendar, a yearly pattern of worship which summarizes and reenacts the events of Christ's life.

3. Specific Church Traditions: the Founders of Denominations and Orders

The Presbyterian Church (U.S.A.) has approximately 2.5 million members, 11,200 congregations and 21,000 ordained ministers. Presbyterians trace their history to the 16th century and the Protestant Reformation. Our heritage, and much of what we believe, began with the French lawyer John Calvin (1509-1564), whose writings crystallized much of the Reformed thinking that came before him.

~ The Presbyterian Church, U.S.A.

Christians have expressed their faith in Jesus Christ in various ways through specific movements and traditions which embrace and express the Authoritative Tradition and the Great Tradition in unique ways. For instance,

[2] *See Appendix B, "Defining the Great Tradition."*

[3] *Even the more radical wing of the Protestant reformation (Anabaptists) who were the most reluctant to embrace the creeds as dogmatic instruments of faith, did not disagree with the essential content found in them. "They assumed the Apostolic Creed–they called it 'The Faith,' Der Glaube, as did most people." See John Howard Yoder,* **Preface to Theology: Christology and Theological Method.** *Grand Rapids: Brazos Press, 2002. pp. 222-223.*

Traditions (continued)

Catholic movements have arisen around people like Benedict, Francis, or Dominic, and among Protestants people like Martin Luther, John Calvin, Ulrich Zwingli, and John Wesley. Women have founded vital movements of Christian faith (e.g., Aimee Semple McPherson of the Foursquare Church), as well as minorities (e.g., Richard Allen of the African Methodist Episcopal Church or Charles H. Mason of the Church of God in Christ, who also helped to spawn the Assemblies of God), all which attempted to express the Authoritative Tradition and the Great Tradition in a specific way consistent with their time and expression.

The emergence of vital, dynamic movements of the faith at different times and among different peoples reveal the fresh working of the Holy Spirit throughout history. Thus, inside Catholicism, new communities have arisen such as the Benedictines, Franciscans, and Dominicans; and outside Catholicism, new denominations have emerged (Lutherans, Presbyterians, Methodists, Church of God in Christ, etc.). Each of these specific traditions have "founders," key leaders whose energy and vision helped to establish a unique expression of Christian faith and practice. Of course, to be legitimate, these movements must adhere to and faithfully express both the Authoritative Tradition and the Great Tradition. Members of these specific traditions embrace their own unique practices and patterns of spirituality, but these unique features are not necessarily binding on the Church at large. They represent the unique expressions of that community's understanding of and faithfulness to the Authoritative and Great Traditions.

Specific traditions seek to express and live out this faithfulness to the Authoritative and Great Traditions through their worship, teaching, and service. They seek to make the Gospel clear within new cultures or sub-cultures, speaking and modeling the hope of Christ into new situations shaped by their own set of questions posed in light of their own unique circumstances. These movements, therefore, seek to contextualize the Authoritative tradition in a way that faithfully and effectively leads new groups of people to faith in Jesus Christ, and incorporates those who believe into the community of faith that obeys his teachings and gives witness of him to others.

Appendix B

Defining the "Great Tradition"

The Great Tradition (sometimes called the "classical Christian tradition") is defined by Robert E. Webber as follows:

> *[It is] the broad outline of Christian belief and practice developed from the Scriptures between the time of Christ and the middle of the fifth century*

~ Webber. **The Majestic Tapestry**.
Nashville: Thomas Nelson Publishers, 1986. p. 10.

This tradition is widely affirmed by Protestant theologians both ancient and modern.

> *Thus those ancient Councils of Nicea, Constantinople, the first of Ephesus, Chalcedon, and the like, which were held for refuting errors, we willingly embrace, and reverence as sacred, in so far as relates to doctrines of faith, for they contain nothing but the pure and genuine interpretation of Scripture, which the holy Fathers with spiritual prudence adopted to crush the enemies of religion who had then arisen.*

~ John Calvin. **Institutes**. IV, ix. 8.

> *. . . most of what is enduringly valuable in contemporary biblical exegesis was discovered by the fifth century.*

~ Thomas C. Oden. **The Word of Life**.
San Francisco: HarperSanFrancisco, 1989. p. xi

> *The first four Councils are by far the most important, as they settled the orthodox faith on the Trinity and the Incarnation.*

~ Philip Schaff. **The Creeds of Christendom**. Vol. 1.
Grand Rapids: Baker Book House, 1996. p. 44.

Our reference to the Ecumenical Councils and Creeds is, therefore, focused on those Councils which retain a widespread agreement in the Church among Catholics, Orthodox, and Protestants. While Catholic and Orthodox share common agreement on the first seven councils, Protestants tend to affirm and use primarily the first four. Therefore, those councils which continue to be shared by the whole Church are completed with the Council of Chalcedon in 451.

It is worth noting that each of these four Ecumenical Councils took place in a pre-European cultural context and that none of them were held in Europe. They were councils of the whole Church and they reflected a time in which Christianity was primarily an eastern religion in it's geographic core. By modern reckoning, their participants were African, Asian, and European. The councils reflected a church that ". . . has roots in cultures far distant from Europe and preceded the development of modern European identity, and [of which] some of its greatest minds have been African" (Oden, *The Living God*, San Francisco: HarperSanFrancisco, 1987, p. 9).

Perhaps the most important achievement of the Councils was the creation of what is now commonly called the Nicene Creed. It serves as a summary statement of the Christian faith that can be agreed on by Catholic, Orthodox, and Protestant Christians.

The first four Ecumenical Councils are summarized in the following chart:

Name/Date/Location	Purpose
First Ecumenical Council 325 A.D. Nicea, Asia Minor	Defending against: *Arianism* Question answered: *Was Jesus God?* Action: *Developed the initial form of the Nicene Creed to serve as a summary of the Christian faith*
Second Ecumenical Council 381 A.D. Constantinople, Asia Minor	Defending against: *Macedonianism* Question answered: *Is the Holy Spirit a personal and equal part of the Godhead?* Action: *Completed the Nicene Creed by expanding the article dealing with the Holy Spirit*
Third Ecumenical Council 431 A.D. Ephesus, Asia Minor	Defending against: *Nestorianism* Question answered: *Is Jesus Christ both God and man in one person?* Action: *Defined Christ as the Incarnate Word of God and affirmed his mother Mary as* **theotokos** *(God-bearer)*
Fourth Ecumenical Council 451 A.D. Chalcedon, Asia Minor	Defending against: *Monophysitism* Question answered: *How can Jesus be both God and man?* Action: *Explained the relationship between Jesus' two natures (human and Divine)*

APPENDIX 14

From Deep Ignorance to Credible Witness

Rev. Dr. Don L. Davis

Witness - Ability to give witness and teach
2. Tim. 2.2
Matt. 28.18-20
1 John 1.1-4
Prov. 20.6
2 Cor. 5.18-21

And the things you have heard me say in the presence of many witnesses entrust to reliable men who will also be qualified to teach others. - 2 Tim. 2.2

8

Lifestyle - Consistent appropriation and habitual practice based on beliefs
Heb. 5.11-6.2
Eph. 4.11-16
2 Pet. 3.18
1 Tim. 4.7-10

And Jesus increased in wisdom and in stature, and in favor with God and man. - Luke 2.52

7

Demonstration - Expressing conviction in corresponding conduct, speech, and behavior
James 2.14-26
2 Cor. 4.13
2 Pet. 1.5-9
1 Thess. 1.3-10

*Nevertheless, at your word I will let down the net.
- Luke 5.5*

6

Conviction - Committing oneself to think, speak, and act in light of information
Heb. 2.3-4
Heb. 11.1, 6
Heb. 3.15-19
Heb. 4.2-6

*Do you believe this?
- John 11.26*

5

Discernment - Understanding the meaning and implications of information
John 16.13
Eph. 1.15-18
Col. 1.9-10
Isa. 6.10; 29.10

*Do you understand what you are reading?
- Acts 8.30*

4

Knowledge - Ability to recall and recite information
2 Tim. 3.16-17
1 Cor. 2.9-16
1 John 2.20-27
John 14.26

*For what does the Scripture say?
- Rom. 4.3*

3

Interest - Responding to ideas or information with both curiosity and openness
Ps. 42.1-2
Acts 9.4-5
John 12.21
1 Sam. 3.4-10

*We will hear you again on this matter.
- Acts 17.32*

2

Awareness - General exposure to ideas and information
Mark 7.6-8
Acts 19.1-7
John 5.39-40
Matt. 7.21-23

*At that time, Herod the tetrarch heard about the fame of Jesus.
- Matt. 14.1*

1

Ignorance - Unfamiliarity with information due to naivete, indifference, or hardness
Eph. 4.17-19
Ps. 2.1-3
Rom. 1.21; 2.19
1 John 2.11

*Who is the Lord that I should heed his voice?
- Exod. 5.2*

0

APPENDIX 15

The Sojourner's Quest

Don L. Davis

Sojourning as pilgrims on a quest to see the Great King
To share the same core, the same hope, the same dream

Walking should-to-shoulder, every burden we bear
With patient conviction, with warmth and great care

In friendship with Christ, our Glory and Crown
That in him alone our real joy would be found

To see with new eyes ev'ry single soul's worth
To cherish the least of these above all else on earth

To burn with deep longing that his praises might flow
And through our sweet unity his beauty might show

Yes, this is our goal, our glory, our aim
That Christ might be seen on this earth once again
That his Kingdom and glory would be powerfully known
That more of his likeness through us might be shown
That for the sake of our friends we would lay down our lives
That his fruit might be borne, and his grace multiplied
That by sharing in common our lights would so shine
That the world might be drawn to him, one heart at a time
And every broken vessel, however humble or meek
Might taste our Lord's mercies, be healed, and set free.

We count now as dung all this world's sweetest pleasures
We press toward the goal for the Kingdom's true treasures
We invite you to join us in our glorious quest
To sojourn with us gladly to his coronation, as guest
We give all that we are and we have to one thing-
To dine soon at his banquet before Christ the Great King.

APPENDIX 16
The Profile of a 21st-Century Disciple
Rev. Dr. Don L. Davis

1. **He/she enjoys an intimate communion with the Lord (John 10.1-6; 15.12-14).**

   a. Is unconditionally available to Christ as Lord (filled with the Holy Spirit)

   b. Hungers to become more and more like Christ in vision, character, and service

   c. Solid devotional life of personal worship, meditation, and prayer

   d. Lifestyle of praise, worship, and celebration

   e. Abiding trust in the leading and provision of God in Christ

   f. Glorifies God in the temple of his/her body, mind, and spirit

2. **He/she upholds a believing stance grounded upon a biblical vision of Christ and his Kingdom (John 8.31-32).**

   a. Thorough understanding of the Holy Scriptures (i.e. its themes, history, and key principles)

   b. Maintains a Christ-centered world view, seeing life from God's vantage point

   c. Grounded in the fundamentals of the faith, able to share and reproduce them

   d. Growing ability to rightly divide the Word of truth (i.e. hear, read, study, memorize, and meditate)

   e. Increasing competence to contend for the faith against all opposition

3. **He/she displays a godly walk through conduct and lifestyle at home, on the job and in the community (John 17.14-23).**

   a. Walks worthy of the Lord in speech, purity, conduct, faith, and character

   b. Fulfills sacrificially various roles as a godly member of his/her own household and family

   c. Represents Christ in excellence, service, respect, and single-mindedness on the job

   d. Maintains godly reputation with friends, neighbors, and community

The Profile of a 21st-Century Disciple (continued)

4. He/she maintains a faithful membership in the body, expressed in active participation in a local congregation of believers (John 13.34-35).

a. Has been baptized into the faith based on their confession of faith in Jesus Christ

b. Participates actively in corporate worship and celebration of the body in praise, worship, and the Lord's Supper

c. Gathers regularly with other members of the body to build up the church through fellowship, prayer, service, and celebration

d. Uses his/her gifts in ministry by serving with other members of the body

e. Communicates regularly in a building and edifying way with the body

5. He/she implements a compelling strategy to make disciples of Jesus at home and abroad (John 20.21).

a. Prays consistently and fervently that the Lord would raise up laborers in his harvest wherever Christ is not yet known, worshiped, and glorified

b. Gives generously of his/her time and resources toward evangelism and missions as God leads

c. Looks for opportunities to share his/her personal testimony with others in order to win others to Christ

d. Spends time establishing new converts in the faith by incorporating them in the body

e. Asks the Spirit for opportunity to disciple faithful Christians who can become laborers together with him/her in fulfilling the Great Commission

APPENDIX 17
Theories of Inspiration
Rev. Terry G. Cornett

Theory of Inspiration	Explanation	Possible Objection(s)
Mechanical or Dictation	The human author is a passive instrument in God's hands. The author simply writes down each word as God speaks it. This direct dictation is what protects the text from human error.	The books of Scripture show diverse writing styles, vocabularies, and manners of expression which vary with each human author. This theory doesn't seem to explain why God would use human authors rather than giving us a direct written word from himself.
Intuition or Natural	Gifted people with exceptional spiritual insight were chosen by God to write the Bible	The Bible indicates that Scripture came from God, through human authors (2 Pet. 1.20-21).
Illumination	The Holy Spirit heightened the normal capacities of human authors so that they had special insight into spiritual truth.	The Scriptures indicate that the human authors expressed the very words of God ("Thus saith the Lord" passages; Rom. 3.2.)
Degrees of Inspiration	Certain parts of the Bible are more inspired than others. Sometimes this position is used to argue that portions dealing with key doctrines or ethical truths are inspired while portions dealing with history, economics, culture, etc. are less inspired or not inspired.	The biblical authors never indicate that some of Scripture is more inspired or treat only one kind of biblical material as inspired in their use of it. Jesus speaks about the entire scriptural revelation up to his day as an unchanging word from God (Matt. 5.17-18; John 3.34-35).
Verbal-Plenary	Both divine and human elements are present in the production of Scripture. The entire text of Scripture, including the words, are a product of the mind of God expressed in human terms and conditions, through human authors that he foreknew (Jer. 1.5) and chose for the task.	It seems unlikely that the human elements which are finite and culture-bound could be described as the unchanging words of God.

APPENDIX 18

Suffering: The Cost of Discipleship and Servant-Leadership

Don L. Davis

To be a disciple is to bear the stigma and reproach of the One who called you into service (2 Tim. 3.12). Practically, this may mean the loss of comfort, convenience, and even life itself (John 12.24-25).

All of Christ's Apostles endured insults, rebukes, lashes, and rejections by the enemies of their Master. Each of them sealed their doctrines with their blood in exile, torture, and martyrdom. Listed below are the fates of the Apostles according to traditional accounts.

- Matthew suffered martyrdom by being slain with a sword at a distant city of Ethiopia.

- Mark expired at Alexandria, after being cruelly dragged through the streets of that city.

- Luke was hanged upon an olive tree in the classic land of Greece.

- John was put in a caldron of boiling oil, but escaped death in a miraculous manner, and was afterward branded at Patmos.

- Peter was crucified at Rome with his head downward.

- James, the Greater, was beheaded at Jerusalem.

- James, the Less, was thrown from a lofty pinnacle of the temple, and then beaten to death with a fuller's club.

- Bartholomew was flayed alive.

- Andrew was bound to a cross, whence he preached to his persecutors until he died.

- Thomas was run through the body with a lance at Coromandel in the East Indies.

- Jude was shot to death with arrows.

- Matthias was first stoned and then beheaded.

- Barnabas of the Gentiles was stoned to death at Salonica.

- Paul, after various tortures and persecutions, was at length beheaded at Rome by the Emperor Nero.

APPENDIX 19

Getting a Firm Grasp of Scripture

*From Leroy Eims, **The Lost Art of Disciple Making**, p. 81*

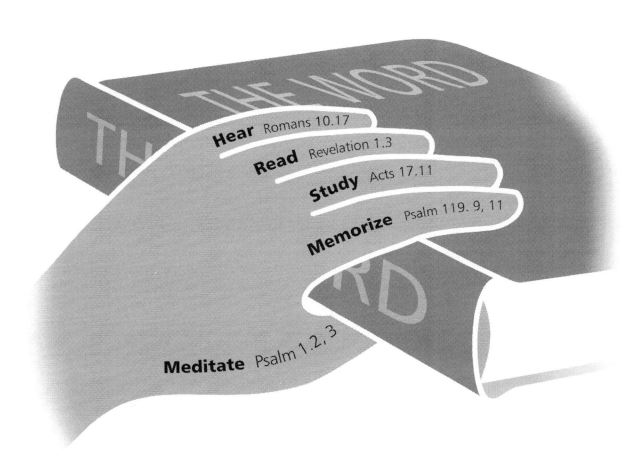

Hear Romans 10.17

Read Revelation 1.3

Study Acts 17.11

Memorize Psalm 119. 9, 11

Meditate Psalm 1.2, 3

APPENDIX 20

Documenting Your Work
A Guide to Help You Give Credit Where Credit Is Due
The Urban Ministry Institute

Plagiarism is using another person's ideas as if they belonged to you without giving them proper credit. In academic work it is just as wrong to steal a person's ideas as it is to steal a person's property. These ideas may come from the author of a book, an article you have read, or from a fellow student. The way to avoid plagiarism is to carefully use "notes" (textnotes, footnotes, endnotes, etc.) and a "Works Cited" section to help people who read your work know when an idea is one you thought of, and when you are borrowing an idea from another person.

Avoiding Plagiarism

A citation reference is required in a paper whenever you use ideas or information that came from another person's work.

All citation references involve two parts:

- Notes in the body of your paper placed next to each quotation which came from an outside source.

- A "Works Cited" page at the end of your paper or project which gives information about the sources you have used

Using Citation References

There are three basic kinds of notes: parenthetical notes, footnotes, and endnotes. At The Urban Ministry Institute, we recommend that students use parenthetical notes. These notes give the author's last name(s), the date the book was published, and the page number(s) on which you found the information. Example:

Using Notes in Your Paper

> In trying to understand the meaning of Genesis 14.1-24, it is important to recognize that in biblical stories "the place where dialogue is first introduced will be an important moment in revealing the character of the speaker . . ." (Kaiser and Silva 1994, 73). This is certainly true of the character of Melchizedek who speaks words of blessing. This identification of Melchizedek as a positive spiritual influence is reinforced by the fact that he is the King of Salem, since Salem means "safe, at peace" (Wiseman 1996, 1045).

Creating a Works Cited Page

A "Works Cited" page should be placed at the end of your paper. This page:

- lists every source you quoted in your paper

- is in alphabetical order by author's last name

- includes the date of publication and information about the publisher

The following formatting rules should be followed:

1. Title

The title "Works Cited" should be used and centered on the first line of the page following the top margin.

2. Content

Each reference should list:

- the author's full name (last name first)

- the date of publication

- the title and any special information (Revised edition, 2nd edition, reprint) taken from the cover or title page should be noted

- the city where the publisher is headquartered followed by a colon and the name of the publisher

3. Basic form

- Each piece of information should be separated by a period.

- The second line of a reference (and all following lines) should be indented.

- Book titles should be underlined (or italicized).

- Article titles should be placed in quotes.

Example:

Fee, Gordon D. 1991. *Gospel and Spirit: Issues in New Testament Hermeneutics.* Peabody, MA: Hendrickson Publishers.

Documenting Your Work (continued)

4. Special Forms

A book with multiple authors:

> Kaiser, Walter C., and Moisés Silva. 1994. *An Introduction to Biblical Hermeneutics: The Search for Meaning.* Grand Rapids: Zondervan Publishing House.

An edited book:

> Greenway, Roger S., ed. 1992. *Discipling the City: A Comprehensive Approach to Urban Mission.* 2nd ed. Grand Rapids: Baker Book House.

A book that is part of a series:

> Morris, Leon. 1971. *The Gospel According to John.* Grand Rapids: Wm. B. Eerdmans Publishing Co. The New International Commentary on the New Testament. Gen. ed. F. F. Bruce.

An article in a reference book:

> Wiseman, D. J. "Salem." 1982. In *New Bible Dictionary.* Leicester, England - Downers Grove, IL: InterVarsity Press. Eds. I. H. Marshall and others.

(An example of a "Works Cited" page is located on the next page.)

For Further Research

Standard guides to documenting academic work in the areas of philosophy, religion, theology, and ethics include:

Atchert, Walter S., and Joseph Gibaldi. 1985. *The MLA Style Manual.* New York: Modern Language Association.

The Chicago Manual of Style. 1993. 14th ed. Chicago: The University of Chicago Press.

Turabian, Kate L. 1987. *A Manual for Writers of Term Papers, Theses, and Dissertations.* 5th edition. Bonnie Bertwistle Honigsblum, ed. Chicago: The University of Chicago Press.

Works Cited

Fee, Gordon D. 1991. *Gospel and Spirit: Issues in New Testament Hermeneutics*. Peabody, MA: Hendrickson Publishers.

Greenway, Roger S., ed. 1992. *Discipling the City: A Comprehensive Approach to Urban Mission*. 2nd ed. Grand Rapids: Baker Book House.

Kaiser, Walter C., and Moisés Silva. 1994. *An Introduction to Biblical Hermeneutics: The Search for Meaning*. Grand Rapids: Zondervan Publishing House.

Morris, Leon. 1971. *The Gospel According to John*. Grand Rapids: Wm. B. Eerdmans Publishing Co. *The New International Commentary on the New Testament*. Gen. ed. F. F. Bruce.

Wiseman, D. J. "Salem." 1982. In *New Bible Dictionary*. Leicester, England-Downers Grove, IL: InterVarsity Press. Eds. I. H. Marshall and others.

Made in the USA
Columbia, SC
21 December 2022

74548230R00091